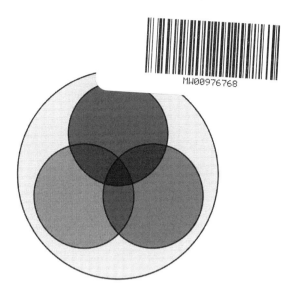

THE
CHURCH:
A MISSIONAL
COMMUNITY

CLEAR CREEK  RESOURCES

LEAGUE CITY, TEXAS

TABLE OF CONTENTS

INTRODUCTION |

...and on this rock I will build my church,
and the gates of hell shall not prevail against it.
- Matthew 16:18

CHURCH, COMMUNITY and MISSION

The church is a community on a mission. It's not just any community. It's not just any mission. Both center upon and revolve around God and the great Good News (or gospel) he offers in Jesus! Over the next several weeks this study will seek to identify and explain exactly how Clear Creek Community Church exists as a missional community. You will read about who we are, what we believe and how we seek to follow Christ together as the local church. In fact, the picture of the church as a missional community can be seen through the lenses of four committed relationships:

- Christ
- The church leadership
- The church community
- The unchurched

These are *missional relationships* to which we must commit in order to fulfill the church's God-given mission. The first three deal with reciprocal relationships found within the local church; the last is the relational context necessary for the church to accomplish her mission of leading others to become fully devoted followers of Jesus. We illustrate it this way:

In order for the church to best accomplish her mission, the individuals who compose the church must be committed to:

- **Christ**, who is the head of the local church
- The **leadership** of the local church
- The **community** that is the local church
- The **unchurched** the local church is attempting to reach

These commitments must be held in order to best grow as followers of Jesus and succeed in fulfilling the mission of helping the unchurched explore, connect and experience Jesus as Savior and Lord.

What was true 2,000 years ago remains true today. In order to honor God through the local church, a Christian must be committed to the same four relationships. This workbook is designed to help you better understand the essence of a believer's relationship with the church community, the church leadership, Christ himself and those he has called us to reach, the unchurched. These commitments are seen in the corresponding statements: *I Belong, I Support, I Believe,* and *I Go.*

DIFFERENT PLACES ON THE JOURNEY
This may excite many of us, but there may be some who might wonder:

> *But what if I'm not a Christian? What if I'm here to check out who Jesus is and what it means to be a Christian? I'm not ready to commit to anything! Small group is a big enough step for me to start with!*

We definitely understand, and realize our small groups are composed of people from different backgrounds spiritually...even no background for some. That's okay. Indeed, we're excited you have chosen to include us in your journey! Our hope is that over the next several studies you will discover much more about Jesus, his church, and that your small group will become a safe place to ask questions and find answers.

Feel free to proceed at your own pace. We don't want you to feel compelled to always answer questions you may not be sure about. In fact, you might find yourself saying to your group, "I'm going to pass on this question because I'm not too sure what I think about it. I need more time to process." Please know, that's the kind of honest, reflective involvement that makes group work! You should also know you're not alone. We will not walk at the same pace or arrive at the same place, but in group we travel together to understand this missional community called the church.

CONCLUSION: YOUR RESPONSIBILITY
This means, regardless of where you are on the spiritual spectrum, you play your part on the journey each week when you:

STEP 1: READ THE STUDY

Take your time and actively read the teaching material each week. Grab a highlighter or pen! Mark up your workbook. Make notes, jot down questions, note sentences or paragraphs that stand out to you.

STEP 2: REFLECT ON THE TEACHING

The "Reflect" section is composed of questions. Your navigator will likely use these questions to guide the group discussion.

STEP 3: READY YOURSELF FOR GROUP

As the time for your group gets closer, periodically pick up the workbook and review the study. Write down any new questions or insights you have. Most of all, pray for group. Ask God to bless your time together, open the hearts of everyone and demonstrate his power during your time together.

SUMMARY – INTRODUCTION

- The local church is a missional community. It is a group of people God has called together to serve his mission in the world.
- A missional community can best be described as a commitment to four relationships – to Christ, church leadership, church community and unchurched.
- The first three are reciprocal relationships. The last is the relational context of our mission.
- All of us are in different places in our spiritual journey. Some may be seasoned Christians while others may not believe at all. This means everyone won't experience this study the same way, and that is okay.
- Your responsibility is to work through the study each week, come prepared, and be ready to engage your group!

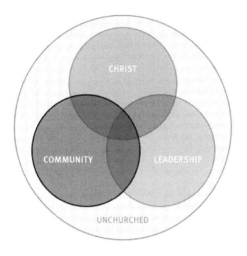

"I BELONG" | WK 2

OUR RELATIONSHIP WITH COMMUNITY

There is one body and one Spirit—just as you were called to the one hope that belongs to your call—one Lord, one faith, one baptism, one God and Father of all, who is over all and through all and in all.

- Ephesians 4:4-6

READ

GOD AND COMMUNITY

God is about community. Indeed, he always has been. Think about how God exists as Trinity or Three-Persons-In-One. It is a mystery to be sure, but it also reveals that God enjoys perfect, eternal fellowship as Father, Son and Spirit. Therefore, community is not just a value he holds, it is who he is. Dr. Timothy Keller writes,

> *The Triune Christian God is the only God who is a community. If God was eternally uni-personal, then love would be something that even God only knew secondarily, after he began to create other beings. But since God is tri-personal, love and friendship are intrinsic to ultimate reality.*[1]

Did you catch that? Our life is to be about community since God is about community. All one has to do is to look at who God is to be convinced. This leads us to a wonderful truth that weaves together God, people and community.

The Bible reveals that Jesus did not die merely to save individuals but to redeem a people to God (cf., Ex. 6:7, Ezek. 37:27, Rev. 21:3). Christ's work at the Cross created a new community composed of those who, throughout history, trust in him as Savior and Lord. This new, gospel-centered community is known as the church.

Jesus said this new community, which was to model for the world what life is like under the rule of God, was to

---

[1] Timothy Keller, <u>Gospel Christianity: Course One</u>, Redeemer Presbyterian Church, 112.

be fueled by a love for God and each other. Jesus told his followers in John 13:34-35,

> *A new commandment I give to you, that you love one another: just as I have loved you, you also are to love one another. By this all people will know that you are my disciples, if you have love for one another.*

This love can only be exhibited in real time, involved relationships – in a word, community! Look at how the early church existed as this type of God-redeemed, loving community:

> *And they devoted themselves to the apostles' teaching and the fellowship, to the breaking of bread and the prayers. And awe came upon every soul, and many wonders and signs were being done through the apostles. And all who believed were together and had all things in common. And they were selling their possessions and belongings and distributing the proceeds to all, as any had need.* (Acts 2:42-45)

This passage helps us see that from the very beginning God's heart for our spiritual growth always has people attached to it. There are no spiritual Lone Rangers. We live as followers of Jesus in community. We must belong! The New Testament paints compelling pictures of how individuals of this gospel-centered community relate to each other:

- Honor one another (Rom. 12:17)
- Accept one another (Rom. 15:7)
- Bear with one another (Col. 3:12-13)
- Forgive one another (Eph. 4:2, 32)
- Pray for and confess to one another (Jam. 5:16)
- Encourage and challenge one another (Heb. 3:13)
- Admonish and confront one another (Rom. 15:14; Gal. 6:1-6)
- Warn one another (1 Thess. 5:14)
- Instruct one another (Col. 3:16)

THE NEED FOR SMALL GROUP

Small group is important at CCCC because it provides a way for us to practice the "one anothers." Small group provides the best relational context for soul-nourishing, spiritually-dynamic community. It is the place where you can know and be known, love and be loved, serve and be served, celebrate and be celebrated. It is where you proclaim to the rest of the church, "I belong!"

Four values permeate the small group experience.

1. Group should be <u>PREDICTABLE</u> – Meeting regularly in a consistent environment for the purpose of growing to be fully devoted followers of Jesus Christ.

2. Group should be <u>INTENTIONAL</u> – Groups exist to help people become fully devoted followers of Jesus Christ through a planned approach to spiritual formation.

GROUPS AND GOSPEL-CENTERED GROWTH
At CCCC we want to emphasize that a Christian's spiritual growth is always anchored to the Person and Work of Jesus (i.e., the gospel). We are currently redesigning our future materials to reflect this truth. The Spiritual Growth Grid (below) is the heart of our spiritual formation process. The grid is composed of three gospel-centered storylines based upon who God is and what he has done for us in the gospel of Jesus and, consequently, who we are and what we do in Christ.

SPIRITUAL GROWTH GRID

REPENT & BELIEVE

WHO GOD IS	WHAT GOD DOES	WHO WE ARE	WHAT WE DO
KING	CALLED	CITIZENS	LISTEN & OBEY
FATHER	ADOPTED	FAMILY	LOVE & SERVE
SAVIOR	SENT	MISSIONARIES	GO & MULTIPLY

Notice that, in Christ, followers of Jesus are citizens who, because of a new allegiance, listen and obey God. They are family members who, because of a new responsibility, love and serve the church. They are also missionaries who, because of a new purpose, go and multiply in the world. Each identity in Christ has a corresponding activity. The Spiritual Growth Grid is CCCC's intentional approach to making fully devoted followers of Jesus in small groups and will be more fully integrated into groups in the near future.

3. Group should be <u>SUSTAINABLE</u> – Practicing life in a community at a pace that allows for small group relationships, corporate worship, serving God in the church and evangelism in the community.

4. Group should be <u>ACCOUNTABLE</u> – Taking reasonable responsibility for each other's spiritual growth and physical well-being.

GROUPS AND CARE

All groups are spiritually accountable to one another. Each group should devise a plan as to how that accountability will look for their specific group. For example, a co-ed group may separate into men and women toward the end of the group time in order to more freely share their joys and struggles spiritually.

Also, groups are the frontline of care at CCCC. Some models of ministry designate the senior pastor (or other members of the church staff) as the one to visit church members who are hospitalized or in need of other pastoral care issues. However at CCCC, the small group is the primary provider of care. This makes sense since few relationships are as closely connected to a person as his or her group. Therefore being a part of a small group is very important. Indeed, we believe CCCC cannot adequately care for someone unless he or she is in a small group.

MAKING GROUP WORK

You contribute to making your group work when you commit to faithfully attending, arriving promptly, being prepared and actively participating. Every person in the group needs to "stack hands" on what being a good small group member looks like. That's why we have provided **Good Group Habits** in Appendix 4.

ACTION: Read over *Good Group Habits* and be prepared to dialogue about it in group. It's important to get group started on the right foot by establishing good group habits from the very beginning! We hope it helps groups talk about practices that transform good groups into great ones.

Group – it's where you can know and be known, love and be loved, care and be cared for, celebrate and be celebrated. When we do group well by being predictable, intentional, sustainable and accountable, it becomes a life-giving community.

COMMUNITY AND CORPORATE WORSHIP

As we noted earlier, Jesus died not only for individuals, but for a community of people (1 Pt. 2:9-10). We know this community as the church. One of her primary activities is to gather together for the purpose of corporately worshipping God. Colossians 3:16 reads,

> *Let the word of Christ dwell in you richly,*
> *teaching and admonishing one another in*
> *all wisdom, singing psalms and hymns and*
> *spiritual songs, with thankfulness in your*
> *hearts to God.*

In corporate worship we praise God through song, seek him in prayer, and hear him through the teaching of his Word. Corporate worship is also a time where we can renew friendships with those we don't see throughout the week. It is a time to both minister and be ministered to. That's likely the reason the writer of Hebrews exhorts believers to faithfully fellowship with the church – "not neglecting to meet together, as is the habit of some." (Heb. 10:24) That's why, along with small group, when you commit to regularly assemble for corporate worship with other followers of Jesus each week you are saying to those who gather with you, "I belong."

In addition to weekly worship services, CCCC gathers at a service known as *The Gathering*. *The Gathering* meets at different times based on the campus you attend. It differs from the weekend services by allowing followers of Jesus to worship in a manner that weekend services might not afford. Generally speaking, less time is given to teaching and more to singing, strategic prayer, and other elements of corporate worship. *The Gathering* gives our faith community another avenue to worship God with Creekers.

COMMUNITY AND THE LORD'S SUPPER
Since *The Gathering* service creates additional space for more expressions of corporate worship, the Lord's Supper is regularly included. This is a special time for baptized believers of Clear Creek Community Church.

The Apostle Paul writes in 1 Corinthians 11:25, "In the same way also he took the cup, after supper, saying, 'This cup is the new covenant in my blood. Do this, as often as you drink it, in remembrance of me.'" This demonstrates that the Lord's Supper is an ordinance given to us by Jesus to continually proclaim, "I trust and believe in Jesus Christ for my salvation – securing my covenant relationship with God." In taking the Lord's Supper we join with the church throughout history in proclaiming our hope in Christ alone. Scripture tells us that Jesus himself is present with us in the Supper in a very significant way (cf., 1 Cor. 10:16-17).

The Lord's Supper has been a regular part of the Christian community throughout the last two millennia. We see its observance from the very beginning of the church. Acts 2:42 records, "And they devoted themselves to the apostles' teaching and the fellowship, to the breaking of bread and the prayers." The "breaking of bread" is likely shorthand for the Lord's Supper in which Jesus broke the bread (1 Cor. 11:24) before he distributed it to his disciples. Justin Martyr (100-165AD), a leading historian for the early church who was a generation removed from the apostles, recorded what happened at a typical service:

We greet one another with a holy kiss. Then a leader from the believers takes a loaf of bread and a cup of wine; after taking them, he offers up praise to the Father of all things, through the name of the Lord. When he has ended his prayers and thanksgiving, the whole congregation present assents by saying 'amen'. After thanksgiving, the deacons among us distribute it to those who are present...no one is allowed to partake of it unless he believes...For the apostles delivered in the memoirs compiled by them, which are called

*Gospels, that this command was given to them
that Jesus took bread.*[2]

The Lord's Supper has always been a very important part
of the rhythm of Christian faith. From the moment it was
first observed to today, participating in the Lord's Supper
reaffirms our identity as followers of Jesus Christ in the
manner he ordained. We are proclaiming along with the
Church Historical through cup and bread that the gospel
of Jesus Christ is our hope and life!

COMMUNITY AND SERVING
The missional community is characterized by service,
Jesus said in Mark 10:42-45,

> *You know that those who are considered
> rulers of the Gentiles lord it over them, and
> their great ones exercise authority over
> them. But it shall not be so among you. But
> whoever would be great among you must
> be your servant, and whoever would be
> first among you must be slave of all. For
> even the Son of Man came not to be served
> but to serve, and to give his life as a ransom
> for many.*

Serving each other is a hallmark of the church.
Through service we model the heart of Jesus to the

---

[2] Justin Martyr, *Apology addressed to Emperor Antoninus Pius*, translated by L. W.
Bernard, (Cambridge, 1967), 61.

world which he came to save. The church functions on the basis of mutual service. 1 Corinthians 12:4-7, 12 reads:

> *Now there are varieties of gifts, but the same Spirit; and there are varieties of service, but the same Lord; and there are varieties of activities, but it is the same God who empowers them all in everyone. To each is given the manifestation of the Spirit for the common good...For just as the body is one and has many members, and all the members of the body, though many, are one body, so it is with Christ.*

Each follower of Jesus is not only graced with spiritual gifts but called to use those gifts (along with their passions, talents and skills) to serve the "Body" or local church. We also believe this service must extend beyond the church campus into the local community and all over the world. Our hope is that our good deeds will open up doors for the Good News. Galatians 6:10 reminds us, "So then, as we have opportunity, let us do good to everyone, and especially to those who are of the household of faith." However, doing good through serving others can be quite a hill to climb in today's consumer-driven culture.

SMALL GROUP AND SEEKING

> *"Okay, I see the reasons for being a part of group if someone is a believer in Jesus, but what if I'm simply seeking to better understand who Jesus is? How does group intersect my life, if at all? Should I be here?"*

Absolutely! Group is incredibly important for those who might consider themselves spiritual seekers who have yet to embrace the gospel of Christ because it affords you the opportunity to experience first-hand what life looks like when you're connected to followers of Jesus.

We hope that you notice immediately how people are loved, encouraged, challenged and cared for by those in the group. Indeed, we hope that you experience those qualities yourself. We also trust you discover that while these individuals who make up the group are far from perfect, their love and devotion to the one who was perfect for them, Jesus, leads them to genuinely seek to grow deeper in their love for God and neighbor. Being exposed to the grace God sheds upon the group is an incredible help for those trying to learn more about Christianity.

Group is also great for spiritual seekers because it gives them a place to ask questions about the faith. You can seek answers together with your group and not feel the need to have the answer in the next five minutes. You can "walk" together with others, take time to process and really journey with others in understanding who God is and what the gospel is all about.

For those who feel the need for a greater amount of time given to questions about the faith, CCCC provides a small group explicitly for them. We call it *Starting Point. Starting Point* meets at each of our campuses (usually Sunday mornings) and is geared for the spiritual seeker who wants to learn more about Christ and the gospel. So, if you find yourself in these initial weeks of group realizing you want a group wired more for your questions about Christianity, we would encourage you to consider joining *Starting Point*. Registration for *Starting Point* is found at our website under "classes," or you could speak with someone at the Welcome Center of your respective campus.

Hopefully, if you are a spiritual seeker, it won't take long for you to see the value of group. We truly believe that one of the best things for people trying to understand what faith in Jesus is all about is joining a small group. We are glad you're here!

COMMUNITY AND CONSUMERISM

Our culture taints us all with the toxin of consumerism. It threatens community. For some, consumerism influences our perspective on church. Consequently, many view themselves as customers at a worship service. They view their presence the same way they view buying a latte from Starbucks. They don't think of investing in the local church any more than you think you should go behind the counter and wash the mugs and clean the sink after you finish your latte at Starbucks. People with this attitude tend to withhold their money, time, gifts, and experiences from the church because, in their eyes, their presence at the service is the price of admission. They come and go as they please. In other words, these individuals have a transactional relationship with the church.

Then it happens. The phone call comes and an anguished voice asks for help, often demanding from the church the very things they have withheld from the church - time, support, resources, and service. In the crisis, the individual wants the one-way street of consumerism to instantly morph into a freeway of fellowship. It is inevitable that the time will come when every person who relates to the church as a customer will misunderstand and mischaracterize the church as uncaring or unresponsive, because the church cannot respond effectively to them. It isn't that the church doesn't want to respond, but how well can the church respond to someone it doesn't know? Fellowship can't both sprout and blossom in the awkward chaos of a funeral plan or in the grief and anxiety of a waiting room.

Don't think we resent those who choose to have a consumerist relationship with the church, we don't. Again, we realize consumerism affects all of us to one degree or another. For some, it has stained their relationship with the church and kept them from embracing the gospel. That's where we want to help! We intentionally create an environment to share the gospel of Jesus with them. We are glad they come to church because we hope that one day they will really hear the good news of Jesus in a life-changing, mind-renewing way and, as a result, start attending because they want to enjoy and worship God and invest in his mission in the world. We believe that when individuals are truly attracted to God they will be attracted to his people and it will become inconceivable to come and go without seeking to know and be known.

People seeking to be a part of the church as missional community trade the power of the customer for the servant-heartedness of a contributor. It is the price of community. It is the cost of discipleship. Maybe the single most distinguishing characteristic of a missional believer at Clear Creek Community Church is that he or she is a contributor. They are the people who contribute to the mission of the church for the sake of sharing the gospel of Jesus with others.

SUMMARY – "I BELONG"
- Followers of Jesus are called to live in community.
- Small group provides the best relational context for spiritual growth.
- The primary provider of care at CCCC is small group. Thus, if a person at CCCC is not in small group, the church cannot adequately care for him.
- For small group to function well, participants need to commit to good group habits.
- One of the primary activities of the church is gathering for corporate worship.
- The Lord's Supper is how we proclaim our hope in Jesus alone and our identity as people of the New Covenant with God.
- Each follower of Jesus has spiritual gifts that are to be used in service to the "Body" or local church.
- Missional people demonstrate their "belonging" by contributing to the mission of the church for the sake of sharing the gospel.

REFLECT

1. Why is community such an important part of the
   Christian faith?

   _____

   _____

   _____

   _____

   _____

   _____

   _____

   _____

   _____

2. Read the Acts 2:42-45 passage again. What stands
   out to you about the early church?

   _____

   _____

   _____

   _____

_____

_____

_____

_____

_____

3. Which "one another" is the most encouraging to you? Why?

_____

_____

_____

_____

_____

_____

4. Why would a small group of people be the best environment for growing as a follower of Jesus Christ?

_____

_____

_____

_____

_____

_____

_____

5. Which of the small group values are most important to you? Why?

_____

_____

_____

_____

_____

_____

_____

6. What strikes you about the Spiritual Growth Grid and the emphasis on what God has done for us in Christ as the focus for our groups?

_____

_____

_____

7. Why is it important that every small group have an intentional plan for growing spiritually? What happens if groups aren't intentional during the lifecycle of their group?

_____

_____

_____

_____

_____

_____

_____

8. Which of the **Good Group Habits** (see Appendix 4) seems to be the hardest to practice? How can the group ensure that these habits are observed consistently?

_____

_____

_____

_____

_____

_____

_____

_____

9. Why do you think CCCC provides care through groups?

_____

_____

_____

_____

_____

_____

10. Why is corporately worshipping God such an important practice of the church?

_____

_____

_____

_____

_____

_____

_____

_____

_____

_____

11. Why did the church view observance of the Lord's Supper as a "given" for all who claimed to be followers of Jesus?

_____

_____

_____

_____

_____

12. Why should serving characterize those in the church?

_____

_____

_____

_____

_____

_____

_____

13. There are some who expect the church to provide for them everything they have personally withheld from the church. Like a customer, they are a relational one-way street that expects the church to provide "goods & services" regardless of their personal commitment. Do you agree? How is this a "transactional relationship" with the church? How do we best serve a consumer at CCCC?

_____

_____

_____

_____

_____

_____

_____

_____

_____

14. Why is personally committing to community such an important part of being a missional community?

_____

_____

_____

_____

_____

_____

_____

_____

Thanks for taking the time to reflect on the reading. Be prepared to share your reflections at your upcoming small group.

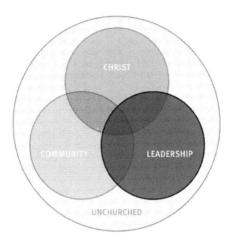

"I SUPPORT" | WK 3

OUR RELATIONSHIP WITH LEADERSHIP

Obey your leaders and submit to them, for they are keeping watch over your souls, as those who will have to give an account. Let them do this with joy and not with groaning, for that would be of no advantage to you.

- Hebrews 13:17

READ

THE NEED FOR LEADERSHIP

That a local church exists and functions implies it has leadership, but it also implies there is "followership". Nothing gets accomplished, personally or organizationally, unless people are willing to follow good leadership. God is a God of order and purpose, so the reason for leadership is simple, someone has to be responsible for setting direction and aligning the church's effort to accomplish its mission. If there is no clear direction there can be a lot of activity with little result – that kind of chaos is contrary to God's very nature. So, a key relational commitment one makes in helping the local church accomplish her mission is to have a God-glorifying relationship with the leadership of the church. In this commitment an individual is saying, "I support!"

God created leadership roles. He calls people into those roles and, as Hebrews 13:17 points out, holds them accountable for how they lead. The Scripture is filled with examples of God's people following the leadership God put in place and how, as Hebrews 13:17 teaches, God instructs the faithful to be submitted to their leaders.

OUR STRUCTURE
The head of Clear Creek Community Church is Jesus Christ. We seek to reflect his priorities in all we do. No decision is ever made that would knowingly contradict his teaching. In addition, through the guidance of the Holy Spirit we seek to discern God's will for us as a church.

On a human level, Clear Creek is structured as follows:

VOLUNTEER-OPERATED
Almost everything that happens at Clear Creek is done through people who invest time and energy to make

our services and ministries possible. We want this local church to fit the apostle Paul's description of the church in Romans 12:5, "...*so we, though many, are one body in Christ, and individually members one of another.*" To experience life in the Kingdom of God means we share the job and joys of proclaiming the gospel and ministering to a community who desperately needs Jesus. A member accepts the mutual responsibility to contribute his or her gifts and energy to the church in a serving role that utilizes one's spiritual gifts and talents. (For more on serving see Week 2)

NAVIGATOR-DISCIPLED
The small group leaders (known as Navigators) are the front line of ministry at Clear Creek. They are the backbone of our mission of helping people become fully devoted followers of Jesus. (For more on small groups see Week 1)

STAFF-LED
The staff of CCCC provide opportunity, equipping, encouragement, and support to people who serve God by doing all the things that need to be done to execute our strategy and accomplish the mission. They are held responsible for their faithful adherence to and execution of the doctrine and direction of the elders.

ELDER-OVERSEEN
The elders are the highest level of authority in the local church (cf., Ac. 14:23, Heb. 13:17, Titus 1:5) and are ultimately responsible for the doctrine, direction and discipline of Clear Creek Community Church.

You can view our staff and elders by visiting the "Who We Are" section of each campus homepage located at www.clearcreek.org.

In addition to this staff structure are the trustees. They do the following:

- Provide financial advice to the elders (at the discretion of the elders)
- Determine the compensation of the Senior Pastor
- Conduct such other duties and activities as the elders may designate from time to time
- Borrow money and incur indebtedness on behalf of CCCC and cause to be executed and delivered for CCCC's purposes and in the CCCC's name, promissory notes and other evidence of debt and securities.

The elders designate the number of trustees who are elected by CCCC members at the annual membership meeting based upon the recommendation of the elders. Each trustee is asked for a one year commitment subject to review, recommitment and reaffirmation by the CCCC membership each subsequent year.

****For a more technical understanding of these offices you can consult the CCCC Bylaws located in **Appendix 9**.*

CHURCH POLITY
Being an elder-overseen congregation means that, unlike local churches which exercise congregational

rule, CCCC is led by a select group of men who give leadership to the doctrine, direction and discipline of the church. The New Testament repeatedly affirms the office and role of elders:

> *So I exhort the elders among you, as a fellow elder and a witness of the sufferings of Christ, as well as a partaker in the glory that is going to be revealed: shepherd the flock of God that is among you, exercising oversight, not under compulsion, but willingly, as God would have you; not for shameful gain, but eagerly; not domineering over those in your charge, but being examples to the flock.* (1 Peter 5:1-3)

> *Pay careful attention to yourselves and to all the flock, in which the Holy Spirit has made you overseers [e.g., elders], to care for the church of God, which he obtained with his own blood.* (Acts 20:28)

> *And when they had appointed elders for them in every church, with prayer and fasting they committed them to the Lord in whom they had believed.* (Acts 14:23)

As an elder-overseen body we do not vote as a congregation on all church issues. Members of CCCC are asked to vote annually on three subjects: 1) the budget; 2) affirmation of elders; 3) election of trustees. All other decisions dealing with the general oversight of the church fall to the elders.

RELATING TO LEADERSHIP

Hebrews 13:17 summarizes the biblical view of this important relationship – the local church elders lead responsibly before God and the church supports and follows their leadership. Thus, when a follower of Jesus commits to a local church as missional community, he is voluntarily submitting to the authority of the leadership of that local church. It means he is committing to follow the elders of that church with respect to the:

- **Doctrine** of the church – the individual affirms CCCC's essential beliefs set forth by the leadership (see Appendix 1), growing in his ability to apply it to his life and agreeing not to teach or promote conflicting doctrine.

- **Direction** of the church – the individual contributes to the mission, values, strategy and culture of the congregation.

- **Discipline** of the church – the individual invites the elders of the local church to assume a spiritual responsibility for him holding him accountable both for living as a disciple of Jesus and actively partnering in accomplishing the mission of the local church.

Let's look at the three aspects in greater depth.

ON DOCTRINE

Let's examine each of these areas as they specifically relate to Clear Creek. Our doctrine is expressed in eight "Essential Beliefs" (see **Appendix 1**). These "essentials" form the basis for how we interpret and apply the Bible, and are non-negotiable beliefs for believers who want to commit to CCCC as a missional community. Those who share our mission should understand and embrace these core beliefs; the beliefs are our doctrinal common ground. We also invite questions and dialogue about the essential beliefs. They are important enough to wrestle with and to understand well.

A good practice would be to overview the beliefs in the appendix while looking up the Scripture references associated with each. This would not only give a clearer perspective on "why" CCCC holds to these beliefs, but would allow you to engage the Bible in a helpful manner.

ON DIRECTION

"Direction" is an important word to us because it encapsulates the mission, vision, values, and strategy of CCCC – it is the what, why, and how of what we do. (For our values see **Appendix 3**.)

Our Mission

Our mission is the reason we exist. It is what makes us a missional community. Thus, everything we do as a church is tied to the mission. Decisions about ministries, programs and the aspects of ministry have their basis and justification in the mission of the church. What's the mission? Jesus gave his church the mission in Matthew 28:19-20,

> *Go therefore and make disciples of all nations, baptizing them in the name of the Father and of the Son and of the Holy Spirit, teaching them to observe all that I have commanded you. And behold, I am with you always, to the end of the age.*

Making disciples of Jesus Christ – that is the mission of the church. It has been the mission of the church for the last 2000 years and will continue to be her mission. Clear Creek Community Church is no different. Our mission is the same:

The mission of Clear Creek Community Church is *to lead unchurched people to become fully devoted followers of Jesus Christ.*

We make it our aim in everything we do to help those far from God come to know him through the person and work of Jesus Christ. Our mission is making disciples – fully devoted followers of Jesus Christ! We will study mission more in-depth in Week 5.

Our Strategy
We have created a strategy to help CCCC accomplish the mission. The strategy is summarized in three phrases: *Explore Faith at Your Campus. Grow Together in Your Group. Make a Difference in Your World.*

- <u>Explore Faith at Your Campus</u> - We try to structure worship services where a complete stranger, experienced or inexperienced in church, will have the greatest opportunity to focus on the gospel of Jesus Christ. Therefore we seek to create an environment where our people, facilities, language, dress and attitude toward each other removes any distractions toward that gospel-end. Worship services can be a place where guests can explore what a faith community committed to the gospel looks like as they gather to worship God, grow in the gospel and seek to live out that gospel not only in their individual lives but in the world around them.

- <u>Grow Together in Your Group</u> - Regardless of how great a worship service is, followers of Jesus cannot begin to reach their potential as disciples if that is the only faith community they experience. Real life change – spiritual growth that produces a gospel-centered heart – occurs most effectively when we engage in a smaller set of relationships with other people who are determined to grow in their devotion to God. Life change happens in small group. The purpose of small group is to provide a set of intentional relationships where people can live out the "one another's"(see Week 1 Study), be known and cared for by other people, and be challenged and held accountable for putting God's truth into practice in their lives.

- <u>Make a Difference in Your World</u> - God didn't wait for us to come to Him, he sent Jesus to bring the promise of a new kind of life to us and make a difference in the world. In the same way, we share the story of how Jesus has changed us, and we want to show the power of his love to people around us. This won't happen unless we're intentional and focus on making a difference. Who are the people in your life that you are going to pray for and reach out to with the message of a better life in Jesus? What would it look like for you to go into their world and show them the love of Jesus? That's what we want to do.

If we are all committed to the strategy of exploring faith, growing together, and going into our communities and the world to make a difference, the life of Jesus will both deepen in our own lives and spread throughout the Bay Area, Houston and beyond.

We Are a Multi-Campus Church
Another aspect of the strategy of Clear Creek is that we are "one church in many neighborhoods". In other words, we are a **multi-campus** church. We have adopted this strategy because we believe that it is best for the gathering place to be located close to the neighbors and friends we are inviting to church. The strategy is to provide empty seats at optimal inviting hours in close proximity to the people we are trying to reach! Every member of CCCC is called on to play a key role in this strategy:

- First, by developing a relationship with and intentionally inviting unchurched friends and neighbors to church.

- Second, by attending and supporting the campus closest to where you live because our friends and neighbors are more likely to attend the closest campus with us.

Once again, all of these decisions and actions (e.g., multi-campus) flow from one source: the mission! For example, the Egret Bay campus had the resources and desire to start a Wednesday Night Service in order to reach people in the Bay Area who couldn't attend services on the weekend. Why? The mission! We are a missional community called by God to lead unchurched people to become fully devoted to Christ. Everything we are about is to glorify God toward this end! We desire to be a church of disciple-making disciples who see their neighborhood, workplace and every other place they find themselves as where God wants to use them to help others embrace the gospel. This is the goal at Clear Creek Community Church for both the leadership and those under that leadership.

ON DISCIPLINE
The obvious key to making this structure work smoothly is the relationship between the leaders and those whom they lead. In a word, there must be unity. 1 Peter 5:1-3 says that elders (and by extension, leaders) are to serve humbly, not domineer over the people in their charge. Accordingly, those under their leadership respond to them in a way that glorifies God,

encourages the leaders and furthers the mission of the church. Hebrews 13:17 clearly spells out this response:

> *Obey your leaders and submit to them, for they are keeping watch over your souls, as those who will have to give an account. Let them do this with joy and not with groaning, for that would be of no advantage to you.*

Much like a dance, there is someone who leads and someone who follows. Both need to do their part – responsibly, faithfully, lovingly. Often that is exactly what happens, and God is greatly glorified. However, there are times when this relationship gets tested.

One of the charges given to the elders is to protect the church from various dangers. They must guard against things such as false teaching and divisive people. Elders also protect the congregation by modeling, guarding and encouraging the biblical standards of godliness. This, at times, includes the administering of church discipline to unrepentant believers. The purpose of church discipline is to be redemptive, seeking the welfare not only of the church in general but the believer in specific.

Theologian Wayne Grudem notes three purposes behind church discipline[3]:

---

[3] Wayne Grudem, *Systematic Theology*, 894-895.

1. Restoration and reconciliation of the believer who is going astray
2. To keep the sin from spreading to others
3. To protect the purity of the church and the honor of Christ

Discipline Begins in Small Group

We must understand that discipline of any matter first begins in the form of small group accountability. Encouraging each other to forsake sin and follow Christ most naturally flows from our personal relationships. Group is composed of individuals committed to love and serve each other while seeking to follow Jesus. Sometimes that means humbly and graciously confronting each other over sin. Jesus taught in Matthew 18:15,

> *If your brother sins against you, go and tell him his fault, between you and him alone. If he listens to you, you have gained your brother.*

More times than not, the path of discipline begins and ends here, resulting in a greater love and trust amongst those who have walked in love and truth together.

Discipline May Involve the Elders

However, sometimes the steps of discipline continue to the elders of the church. Jesus continues in Matthew 18:16-17,

> *But if he does not listen, take one or two others along with you, that every charge may be established by the evidence of two or three witnesses. If he refuses to listen to them, tell it to the church. And if he refuses to listen even to the church, let him be to you as a Gentile and a tax collector.*

In this situation the matter has progressed from a private, informal issue to a public and much more formal process of discipline. If personal sin against someone cannot be resolved in a private or small group meeting, then the matter can be brought "to the church", meaning it would be before the elders. This is a sobering but necessary ministry of the elders. The aim of church discipline is to be redemptive for the erring believer and to uphold God's honor for his missional community. For more information on the CCCC's church discipline policy read **Appendix 5**, or for a more technical description, see **Appendix 9** (Exhibit B).

How does church discipline intersect a commitment to be a part of a missional community? It declares that the person both affirms the leadership of the elders and the biblical role of accountability which accompanies that relationship. It is giving the leadership of CCCC "permission to ask" and follow through on shepherding that individual toward becoming a fully devoted follower of Jesus Christ in community – even if that shepherding necessitates the accountability of church discipline.

THE STRUGGLE TO SUPPORT

Some find it a struggle to support leaders, especially those who have been led poorly. However, there are others who don't want to follow no matter how sterling of leadership is given. They seem, almost by definition, to resist any type of authority, control or tradition. In the arena of church, it is a person who has their own agenda and sets it above the direction set by the elders - while at the same time desiring the resources of the church to pursue their agenda. He subordinates the mission, vision and values of the local church to his own personal mission and values.

It is important to note that this type of individual may have legitimate passions and a true God-given heart for a specific ministry or group of people. It's just that they won't accept any leadership which doesn't share an equal value for the same specific passion or that interferes with how they do what they want to do. As a result they often compete against the local church for its resources. Thus, while they can operate in community as a follower of Christ, they can dilute the energy and focus of the church.

Unfortunately, these individuals consistently are sources of complaints and division because they cannot submit to leadership which does not recognize their particular mission as most important. Or some desire a leadership role simply to create a personal following for themselves within the church. Sadly, they freely criticize the local church leadership in order to promote themselves as more spiritual or better qualified to lead than those currently leading.

Ironically, they may not really have any concerns with the mission or vision of the church, they are just unwilling to submit to authority. In the end, these individuals promote an adversarial relationship with the church, specifically with the church leadership, and can easily become the source of disputes, complaints and a disgruntled spirit in the congregation. They aren't healthy for the church...or themselves.

Those committed to missional community, on the other hand, freely and gladly support the leadership of their church. This support doesn't mean eschewing critical thinking or dialogue with the leadership about ideas, issues or other areas important to the church. On the contrary, CCCC welcomes that kind of active, involved presence. Ultimately however, a missional community is comprised of people who can say with full confidence, "*I support* the elders and leadership of Clear Creek Community Church in accomplishing the mission of making fully devoted followers of Jesus Christ."

SUMMARY – "I SUPPORT

- Having a God-glorifying relationship with the leadership is a key component to a missional community, which means voluntarily submitting to the authority and leadership of the elders in doctrine, direction and discipline.
- The mission of CCCC is *to lead unchurched people to become fully devoted followers of Jesus Christ.* CCCC seeks to do everything for the mission.
- We are a multi-campus church. It is not just what we do. Because of mission, it's who we are.

- CCCC is led by elders, not congregational voting.
- Part of the elders' responsibility to the church concerns discipline.
- Being committed to missional community means inviting the elders to assume a spiritual responsibility for you and hold you accountable to both living as a follower of Jesus and actively partnering in CCCC's mission

REFLECT

1. "A key commitment someone makes when they choose to become a part of a missional community is the commitment to have a God glorifying relationship with the leadership of that church." What happens in a church when this commitment isn't valued?

_____

_____

_____

_____

_____

_____

_____

_____

2. Write your reflections on Hebrews 13:17.

_____

_____

_____

_____

_____

_____

_____

_____

3. Based on CCCC's structure, why are volunteers so important? Explain how this encourages or discourages you?

_____

_____

_____

_____

_____

_____

_____

_____

_____

_____

4. Why do you think we believe that small group
   Navigators are the "backbone of [CCCC's] mission"?
   What does that say about the importance of their
   integrity of following Jesus and facilitating group?

_____

_____

_____

_____

_____

_____

_____

_____

_____

5. Write the mission of CCCC in your own words.

_____

_____

_____

_____

6. If someone were to ask you how they could get
   plugged in at CCCC, what would you tell them?

_____

_____

_____

_____

_____

_____

_____

_____

_____

_____

_____

7. How does being a multi-campus church demonstrate our commitment to the mission? Why and how do you believe people may struggle with this strategy?

_____

_____

_____

_____

_____

_____

_____

_____

_____

8. Are there any **Essential Beliefs** (Appendix 1) you struggle with? Are there other beliefs that you think are essential for membership?

_____

_____

_____

_____

_____

_____

_____

_____

_____

_____

9. What does it mean that CCCC is an elder-overseen church as opposed to a congregational form of church government? Is that different from your prior church experience?

_____

_____

_____

_____

_____

_____

_____

_____

_____

10. "The obvious key to making this structure work smoothly is the relationship between the leaders and those whom they lead. In a word, there must be unity." How can leaders and those who are under their leadership best contribute to the unity under this type of relationship?

_____

_____

_____

_____

_____

_____

_____

_____

_____

_____

11. What does it mean that in committing to the church as missional community we give the elders "permission to ask"?

_____

_____

_____

_____

_____

_____

_____

_____

_____

12. Why should church discipline actually encourage followers of Jesus? What insights did you gather from Dr. Wayne Grudem's comments on church discipline (see Appendix 5) that helped give clarity to this practice?

_____

_____

_____

_____

_____

_____

_____

13. There are some who make commitments to Jesus Christ and the community of faith but not the leadership of the community of faith. How does this

lack of commitment ultimately undermine their professed commitments to the other two spheres (Christ and community)? How is this an adversarial relationship?

_____

_____

_____

_____

_____

_____

_____

_____

_____

_____

_____

_____

Thanks for taking the time to reflect on the reading. Be prepared to share your reflections at your upcoming small group.

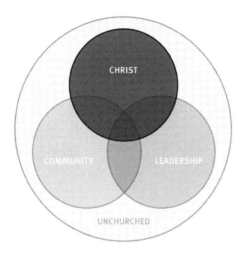

"I BELIEVE" | WK 4

OUR RELATIONSHIP WITH CHRIST

For I delivered to you as of first importance what I also received: that Christ died for our sins in accordance with the Scriptures, that he was buried, that he was raised on the third day in accordance with the Scriptures, and that he appeared to Cephas, then to the twelve.

- 1 Corinthians 15:3-5

READ

The gospel. If you have been around Clear Creek Community Church for any amount of time it is probably something you have heard quite often. Why do we talk about it so much? It is because the gospel is good news for us (the word literally means "good news"). It is why the church exists. Indeed, the reason we are knit together as a body of believers is because we have received God's good news in Jesus Christ. What exactly is this good news?

OUR CONDITION

God created the world as a wonderful place for humanity to enjoy him and the gifts he had given. Yet our first parents, Adam and Eve, did not obey (sinned against) God and brought upon themselves, their descendants and the world a separation from God (Gen. 1-3). In their disobedience the entire human race was stained with sin. We see evidence of this in our lives every day. So from Adam to you, sin has not only alienated us from God but makes us deserving of the penalty of sin – spiritual death or eternal separation from God.

THE WORK OF THE GOSPEL

But instead of leaving us in our eternally perilous condition, God reached out in love through his only Son, Jesus Christ. John 3:16 says,

> *For God so loved the world, that he gave his only Son, that whoever believes in him should not perish but have eternal life.*

Jesus lived his life on earth in perfect obedience to God's Law. Even though Jesus never sinned, never disobeyed God, he died a humiliating death on a Cross to pay for my sin and your sin. Three days after Jesus was buried, he was resurrected and thus conquered sin and death. God offers forgiveness and restoration to those who solely place their trust in Jesus for their salvation. On the cross, Jesus not only bore the full penalty for our sins against a holy God but imputed his perfect righteousness to our account. The gospel, or good news, is that Jesus has become for us what we cannot become for ourselves. He has become our righteousness, our sacrifice and our obedience unto God.

GOD'S OFFER

Through his Son Jesus, God, the Ruler of Creation, proclaims to all who are trying to achieve their salvation through self-merit and good works, "Good news! Your strength, intelligence and morality are inadequate to enter into the kingdom because no one is perfectly righteous. Indeed, all have sinned and fallen short of my standard. But I have offered you forgiveness and entrance into my kingdom through the work of my Son at the Cross." The call of the gospel is to let Jesus become our righteousness, forgiveness and life. It is to let Jesus do for us what we could not do for ourselves.

THE GOSPEL IS NOT A RELIGION

The gospel helps us understand that neither irreligion nor religion are helpful. Indeed, religious people can be just as far from God as someone who has never darkened the doors of a church. Religion incorrectly teaches that morality and goodness gain favor with God and merit salvation, while irreligion preaches a "salvation" through autonomy and personal fulfillment. In the end, both are attempts to control God. Christianity, however, says that salvation isn't based on our morality or achievement but upon God's grace in Jesus Christ. Ephesians 2:8-9 reads:

> *For by grace you have been saved through faith. And this is not your own doing; it is the gift of God, not a result of works, so that no one may boast.*

Salvation through Jesus is given as a free gift to those who respond in faith alone in him. It is all by grace, by God's free and unmerited favor – meaning we can never earn our salvation or contribute to it. We might put it as some in church history have said: *We are saved by grace alone through faith alone in Christ alone.* Good news, indeed! How does this response evidence itself?

RECEIVING CHRIST

Put simply, a person becomes a Christian when he or she turns from his self-ruled life and embraces Jesus Christ, utterly trusting in who he is and what he has done for their salvation. Often that begins with a prayer of repentance and request similar to the following:

> *Dear Father God, I am a sinner. Apart from you I have no hope. Forgive me of my sins. I repent and turn to your gift of the gospel. I now believe in who Jesus is and what he has done – that he is God in the flesh, lived a perfect life I couldn't and died in my place as a substitute for my sins. I also believe that he rose from the grave to demonstrate his victory over sin and death. I am placing*

my faith alone in Christ alone for my salvation. Thank you for the good news of your gospel. In the name of Jesus Christ, my Lord and Savior, I pray. Amen.

While a person's specific words certainly may be different, the heart of this prayer (e.g., confession of sin, believing in who Jesus is and what he has done, asking to receive Christ) remains the same. We receive the good news of God when we place our complete trust in the person and work of Jesus Christ for our salvation. Now we live in the realm of grace. We live "in Christ". We are forever loved, forever forgiven and dwell eternally with God.

BAPTISM

The first act of newly converted followers of Jesus is baptism. It symbolizes our trust in Jesus. In fact, the going in and out of the water parallels the death, burial and resurrection of Jesus. In baptism, we are identifying ourselves with him. If the Lord's Supper is the God-ordained means by which we declare our fidelity to the gospel of Jesus, baptism is the God-ordained means whereby we declare our belief and acceptance of the gospel. This was such an expected practice in the New Testament that the biblical writers often used baptism as shorthand for becoming a Christian. It is also why all throughout the history of the church that only baptized believers were allowed to participate in the Lord's Supper. There is no record in the Scriptures of a Christian who did not seek to be baptized immediately when afforded the opportunity. To not do so would be equivalent to saying, "I have not embraced Jesus as Savior and Lord," or, "I do not want to be a part of the people of God."

This is why baptism is such an important part of Clear Creek Community Church. It is hardwired into our mission given to us by Jesus. He said in Matthew 28:19, "Go therefore and make disciples of all nations, *baptizing* them in the name of the Father and of the Son and of the Holy Spirit..." Every time we baptize someone we are celebrating with them in their proclamation that they have become followers of Jesus and have entered the community of saints known as the Church!

BELIEF AND BAPTISM

It is helpful to note that in the New Testament, baptism always follows belief in Jesus (Ac. 2:38, 41; 8:12-13). In other words, people were baptized after they personally chose to believe in Jesus Christ as Savior and Lord, not at any time before. Consequently, CCCC only baptizes people who have personal faith in Jesus; therefore, infants are not baptized. While infant baptism is often meaningful to parents, the person baptized did not experience scriptural baptism. Believers who have only experienced infant baptism should seek New Testament baptism after coming into a personal relationship with Jesus Christ by faith.

Baptism in the Bible is done by immersion. The word in the New Testament translated baptism actually means "to immerse, or dip under." This seems correct being that immersion adequately symbolizes the death and resurrection we experience in Jesus (Rom. 6:3-4,

Col. 2:12). Those who were baptized in some other way, other than immersion, are encouraged to seek baptism by immersion in keeping with the biblical pattern. However, the mode of baptism (immersion, pouring or sprinkling) is not viewed as an essential matter for membership at Clear Creek Community Church. What is an essential matter for membership is that the baptism occurred *after* placing personal faith in Jesus Christ (see Elders' Perspective on Baptism in Appendix 6).

Belief and baptism. One grants us full entrance into the Body of Christ (i.e., the Church), the other proclaims it for all to see. Ephesians 4:4-6 reads:

> *There is one body and one Spirit—just as you were called to the one hope that belongs to your call—one Lord, one faith, one baptism, one God and Father of all, who is over all and through all and in all.*

This is how those who desire to be a part of a missional community commit to their relationship with Christ. Through word and water we shout, "I believe!" We believe the gospel of grace found only in Jesus Christ!

GETTING FAITH RIGHT

There are many who believe their relationship with God is based on faith in themselves and their ability to "do the right things", not in the saving work of Jesus. They assume since they are good at checking off a bunch of religious boxes they merit God's favor and salvation. So, it is easy for them to follow church leadership because they find their security in their ability to perform responsibilities, affirm doctrines, and generally just live a religious lifestyle. It is also easy for them to be a part of a small group because they are comfortable in religious environments and confident in how they compare spiritually with other people. Unfortunately, while they may be religious and claim the title "Christian", they do not really understand their deep spiritual need for grace through Christ and so do not trust in him for their salvation.

These are dangerous individuals in the church. It is easy for them to be critical and judgmental of other people because they are unwilling to acknowledge any shortcomings in their own life, believing they are doing all the right things to earn God's approval. Consequently, they will make someone who is exploring faith in Jesus or who is new to faith in Jesus feel unwelcome and create an environment where others are unwilling to confess the truth about areas in their lives they need to grow – there is no room for poor performance in their perspective.

Jesus confronted these types of people directly and was harshly critical of them (see John 8 where Jesus confronts the Pharisees.) Like the people Christ confronted, these individuals often have ulterior motives in their relationship with the church. They are not truly seeking to grow their relationship with Christ and glorify God but to further personal agendas such as expanding their business clientele or search for a spouse. Ultimately, they have a utilitarian relationship to the church.

Someone committed to missional community, on the other hand, has given his or her life to Christ and, while not perfect, desires to grow in full devotion in him. He finds his joy in the good news that not only have his sins been completely forgiven by God but he now possesses a new identity in Christ. Jesus is his sufficiency, hope and life. These types of committed individuals continually preach the gospel to themselves in order to be reminded of these wonderful, soul-growing truths! They know that to truly be connected to the church they must be authentically connected to her head – Jesus Christ! Again, those who entrust themselves to missional community gladly proclaim, "I believe!"

SUMMARY – "I BELIEVE"
- All humanity is separated from God but in the gospel, Jesus pays the penalty for our sin that we cannot pay ourselves, and in doing so brings forgiveness to those who trust him by faith alone.
- Baptism is an expected response to receiving the gospel in faith.
- Committing to missional community means having both personally received Christ as Lord and Savior and subsequently baptized as a proclamation of receiving Christ.
- Unfortunately, some individuals have a utilitarian relationship in that they use the church for their own selfish motives. They commit to Community and Leadership but not Christ.

REFLECT

1. Based on the reading, how would you define the gospel?

_____

_____

_____

_____

_____

_____

_____

_____

_____

2. How is the gospel "Good News" for us?

_____

_____

_____

_____

_____

_____

3. What does it mean to say "the gospel is not a religion"? Use Ephesians 2:8-9 to help answer the question.

_____

_____

_____

_____

_____

_____

_____

_____

_____

4. "We are saved by grace alone through faith alone in Christ alone." Why is it important to have the word "alone" in this statement?

_____

_____

_____

_____

5. How do people confuse Christianity with religion (as defined in the reading)?

_____

_____

_____

_____

_____

_____

6. Why is baptism such an important step after someone becomes a follower of Jesus?

_____

_____

_____

_____

_____

_____

_____

_____

25

7. What does "Belief before Baptism" mean and why is it significant for those seeking to commit to CCCC as missional community?

_____

_____

_____

_____

_____

_____

_____

8. What does it mean to have a utilitarian relationship with the church?

_____

_____

_____

_____

_____

_____

_____

9. As a church, how can we guard against producing consumeristic types of attitudes in our congregation?

_____

_____

_____

_____

_____

_____

_____

10. What are ways your small group can continue to be a gospel-centered group?

_____

_____

_____

_____

_____

_____

Thanks for taking the time to reflect on the reading. Be prepared to share your reflections at your upcoming small group.

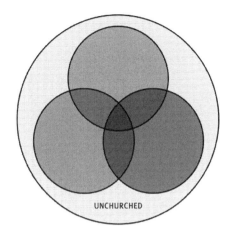

UNCHURCHED

"I GO" | WK 5

OUR RELATIONSHIP WITH THE UNCHURCHED

But you will receive power when the Holy Spirit has come upon you, and you will be my witnesses in Jerusalem and in all Judea and Samaria, and to the end of the earth.

- Acts 1:8

READ

We noted at the very beginning of this study that while the first three committed relationships of a missional community are reciprocal relationships found within the local church; the fourth relationship (the unchurched) is to people in the community who are not part of the church. The church's mission is to lead others to become fully devoted followers of Jesus. This week's study will seek to give understanding as to why CCCC is so committed to the mission of leading unchurched people to become fully devoted followers of Jesus Christ.

A SENDING GOD, A SENT CHURCH

In Week 3 we read in Matthew 28:19 that when Jesus established his church he gave it marching orders: *Go therefore and make disciples of all nations.* The mission of the church was to lead others to become fully devoted followers of Jesus as we are "going" into the world – into our homes, our neighborhoods, our work, our school, our everything! In other words, not only is the church a community which gathers weekly to corporately worship God, but the church is sent out to help others far from God understand and receive the gospel. Thus, the church is a sent people on mission, called and empowered in that mission by a sending God (cf., Acts 1:8). To whom are we sent? The unchurched.

We use the term "unchurched" to describe those who have not embraced the gospel of Jesus Christ because it helps remind us that in order for the mission of God to be accomplished, believers must engage with those outside the church. Our dream is that everyone who considers themselves committed to the church as missional community see themselves as *missionaries.* Sound funny? It doesn't need to. A missionary is simply someone who strategically lives life in order that people far from God will have maximum exposure to the gospel.

That's what we want CCCC to become – a church full of missionaries to the world around us! We want students who are missionaries to their schools, neighbors who are missionaries to their subdivisions and employees who are missionaries to their workplace.

MISSIONAL LIVING

Commitment to the unchurched brings with it an awareness and intentionality to people's lives – they live missionally. In other words, their daily life is always attempting to answer the question: *How can I bring the gospel to those around me through word and deed?*

This question affects everything! It causes us to see with new eyes the "faces and places" God has put before us and how they can be transformed by the gospel. It's a question that moves our lives toward exposing as many as possible to the good news of grace! Living missionally can lead a person to:

- *Engage in a Mercy Ministry*. We believe that God calls us to good deeds (cf., 1 Pt. 2:12). Good deeds can open up doors for the good news. Additionally, when we share mercy with those in need we demonstrate to the world around us that we really do care about them, that God in Christ really does care for them. One of the ways CCCC engages in mercy ministries is through Go Ops. Go Ops are service opportunities done by small groups. Throughout the year, groups feed the homeless, provide clothing for the needy and engage in all kinds of activities geared at loving our communities with the love of Christ. Each small group appoints a Go Catalyst to identify and coordinate Go Ops for the group. You can see what Go Ops are available at *www.clearcreek.org/go*.

- *Take a Go Trip*. Being on foreign soil in the name of Jesus will change your heart. *Go Trips* are CCCC's endeavor at helping those in groups have hands-on mission experiences. We send teams that share Jesus, help plant churches, serve people and make a long-term difference in places around the globe. You can see what Go Trips are currently available at *www.clearcreek.org/go*.

- *Regularly Pray for your Top 5*. We realize that ultimately embracing Christ and the gospel is a work only God can do in the heart. This demands that we pray for our unchurched friends and neighbors. The *Top 5* is a list of the five people you most want to see receive the gospel of Jesus Christ. We ask everyone who desires to live missionally to develop their Top 5 list and regularly pray for them, asking God to bring them to himself and using you as a part of the process. The *Top 5* is also a good reminder of who we should be intentionally trying to develop an authentic relationship with. This is the characteristic of a missional life.

- *Invest and Invite the Unchurched*. Our hope is that countless numbers of the unchurched will attend CCCC and hear the gospel on a weekend because someone cared enough to build a relationship of authenticity with them and subsequently invited them to church. Missional living means intentionally investing in your unchurched relationships, sharing the gospel with them and bringing them on your arm to a weekend service. The odds of attending a worship service increase exponentially when a friend's invitation is in the equation. Missionally-minded people make the "ask" a part of their daily lives.

Can you see how missional living changes our lives? Our hope and prayer is that CCCC can partner along with you to fulfill the mission God has given us of leading the unchurched to become fully devoted followers of Jesus Christ.

A CHURCH FOR THE UNCHURCHED
The mission of reaching the unchurched has always been one of the highest priorities at CCCC. For example, it influences how we conduct services on the weekends. We want to provide a place where not only believers can genuinely worship God but unbelievers can easily investigate the gospel as well. One of the ways we demonstrate that commitment is by trying to reduce barriers for the unchurched. The gospel of grace, which says one is made right with God not by his or her merit but solely by the work of Christ, is barrier enough (cf., 1 Cor. 1:18-31). Therefore, we don't want to place any unnecessary barriers for those who want to know more about Jesus and the gospel when they

come to a service. Here are a few examples of how we have tried to remove barriers.

- *Parking Team* – Our team seeks to help get people parked in a safe and friendly way. Parkers help take some of the stress out of getting into the service on time.

- *Seeker-Sensible Service* – Every community has its own vocabulary. The church is no different and sometimes that can be difficult for the "spiritual seeker" who is investigating Christianity. Consequently, CCCC aims at preaching which speaks plainly, where the messages are easy to understand for the person who does not have much experience with the Bible.

- *Gospel-Centered Service* – We believe that both believer and unbeliever need the gospel. Through faith in the good news of God's grace in Jesus, people are made right with God. We believe the gospel is also central for the Christian life. Thus the services at CCCC aim at keeping the gospel in the middle of it all – the songs, the stories, the sermon, everything! We hope that when you bring your unchurched friend to a service you can trust he or she will be exposed to the good news of Jesus.

- *Multiple Sites* – CCCC is composed of different local campuses because people are most likely to get involved in a church that is closest to where they live. CCCC wants to provide empty seats at optimal inviting hours in close proximity to the people we are trying to reach. The best way to accomplish this is by planting multiple sites around the Bay Area, to be one church in multiple neighborhoods.

These are just a handful of ways CCCC has tried to make the worship service an effective place for the unchurched who desire to know more about Christ. We have unapologetically held the line on being a church for the unchurched because of our commitment as a missional community. Mindful that we can always grow in how we corporately gather for worship, we will continue to ask ourselves how can CCCC continue to accomplish the mission of leading others to become fully devoted followers of Jesus Christ?

BEING MISSIONAL BEYOND OUR COMMUNITY
We also want the mission to the unchurched to reach further than just our own community. Jesus said in Acts 1:8,

> *But you will receive power when the Holy Spirit has come upon you, and you will be my witnesses in Jerusalem and in all Judea and Samaria, and to the end of the earth.*

While specifically fulfilled by the church in the book of Acts, Jesus words can also help give us a framework for thinking about how we reach the unchurched. The missional movement for the early believers was from their own community (Jerusalem) to larger circles of concern ("...*all Judea and Samaria, and to the end of the earth.*"). How does CCCC take the mission to areas outside the immediate Bay Area? The answer is church planting.

We believe planting new churches locally, nationally and internationally is the best strategy for accomplishing the mission of leading unchurched people to become fully devoted followers of Christ. Thus, CCCC is a church-planting church. Our desire is to see thousands of churches planted as a result of our endeavors. Here are some ways CCCC is currently involved in church planting:

- *Multi-site.* Part of planting churches is beginning new CCCC campuses in our local area. Outside of the immediate Bay Area, we focus on new churches.

- *Supporting church planters.* Every year the elders of CCCC select different church planters around the Houston area to support. The support is multi-faceted, including: financial, coaching, and leadership training.

- *Church planting networks.* Partnering with other like-minded churches enables us to accomplish more of the mission than we could do alone. We are affiliated with different church planting networks and organizations, such as the Acts 29 Network and the Houston Church Planting Network. Through these networks, CCCC supports and participates in conferences, trainings and other meetings that increase the effectiveness of church-planting in Houston and around the world.

Hopefully it is becoming clear that CCCC deeply desires to be a missional community, but the only way we can do that effectively is by having a genuine commitment to the unchurched around us. This means that those who want to be active participants in the missional community must personally make this commitment as well. It is a commitment to love those far from God: to reach them, serve them, pray for them, and share the gospel with them. A missional community is committed to Christ, the leaders and the congregation. But unlike those mutual relationships, a missional community is also committed to those who are not committed to them – the unchurched. For an unchurched person, people on-mission will say, "I go!"

GOING WITH THE VISION

We want to conclude this section with a personal letter from Senior Pastor Bruce Wesley:

> *I appreciate you considering partnering with us in the mission of CCCC. Let me tell you about my first encounter with the people who started this church. I hope as you read, you'll better understand our heartbeat as a church.*
>
> *In 1993, Susan and I met with seven people in League City. We gathered in a living room around a cup of coffee and talked about our dreams to start a church together.*

I talked about my passion to be an authentic church that was on mission in the world. A community of believers—yes, but it was a community with a cause. The church is not a country club where membership has its privileges, but a church where membership has its passionate responsibility to individually and corporately follow the leadings of our Commander in Chief, Jesus Christ without regard for what I called the TPC's—traditions, preferences, and comforts. The TPC's were some of the things that kept churches from prevailing in their mission.

Unity grew around the mission of being a church with the priority of leading unchurched people to become fully devoted followers of Christ. We wanted to do church in such a way that our unchurched friends would come and like it. A church for those burned by religion and scarred by sin would have to be a place of grace, a place where it is legal to have problems and legal to talk about them.

We considered how the church is under a mandate from God to act as Jesus acted toward people who were not religious or church goers. Jesus was body #1, he came "to seek and to save that which was lost." And Jesus gave body #2, the body of Christ on earth, the same mission, "to seek and to save that which is lost." So we talked about how we should build relationships with unchurched people and share a natural witness with them. Jesus treated sinners with the dignity due every person created in the image of God. But he spoke truth without compromise while showing love without pretense. We committed ourselves to a church that would remove all non-essential barriers that might run people away from God.

Jesus is worthy of fully devoted followers. 95% devotion to Christ is 5% short. So we determined to create a community where Jesus is worshipped, His Word is honored and we celebrate the way God changes our lives to be more and more like Jesus. We believe that life change happens best in small groups.

We dreamed of an army of small groups penetrating the Bay Area with genuine, loving relationships, a hunger to grow spiritually, a heart to serve others and contagious faith. In groups, no one walks alone. Everyone can have what we call "2AM friends," people close enough to call when you need help in the middle of the night.

We agreed that the church should function with every member being a minister using his or her gifts to serve God and people. The church should be led by leaders, taught by gifted teachers. Administrators should administrate and mercy showers should minister compassion and shepherds should shepherd small groups just like the Bible shows the New Testament church operated. Every believer and member would contribute, by using their spiritual gifts and by giving generously. Then at night, each one would lay his head on his pillow and feel the euphoria of eternal significance because he invested in the things that matter most and last forever.

Healthy churches grow and multiply. So we envisioned starting a church planting movement that would be instrumental in raising up the church leaders of tomorrow and starting new churches close to home and around the world.

In 2006, CCCC became a multi-campus church. When we realized that people who live closest to the church building were more likely to fully engage in the mission of the church, we determined to start new campuses around the Bay Area. We want to provide empty seats at optimal inviting hours in close proximity to the people we are trying to reach.

If your heart beats fast at the thought of being in a church with a dream like this, join us in our mission to lead unchurched people to become fully devoted followers of Christ.

SUMMARY – "I GO"

- The church is a sent people on mission, called and empowered in that mission by a sending God. Because that is so, the unchurched are important to us.
- A missional life asks: *How can I bring the gospel to those around me through word and deed?* Praying for your Top 5, inviting the unchurched to a weekend service, engaging in Go Ops and Go Trips are just some characteristic of living missionally.
- Having a "Seeker-Sensible" worship service means we worship God together aware of the fact that unbelievers (i.e., the *uninitiated*) are in the room and communicate in a way they can understand.
- We are a church planting church committed to multi-site, supporting church planters and networking with other church planting organizations in Houston and around the world.

REFLECT

1. How is God a "sending" God?

_____

_____

_____

_____

_____

_____

2. Why is it important that a missional community have all its committed members view themselves as missionaries?

_____

_____

_____

_____

_____

_____

3. What are ways people on mission can engage in mercy ministries?

_____

_____

_____

_____

_____

_____

_____

4. In the church, what can become potential *unnecessary* barriers to the gospel?

_____

_____

_____

_____

_____

_____

_____

5. Define "seeker sensible" service.

_____

_____

_____

_____

_____

_____

6. How is being multi-campus a commitment to being missional?

_____

_____

_____

_____

_____

_____

_____

_____

7. What is church-planting? How does CCCC
   contribute to church-planting?

_____

_____

_____

_____

_____

_____

_____

_____

_____

_____

Thanks for taking the time to reflect on the reading.
Be prepared to share your reflections at your
upcoming small group.

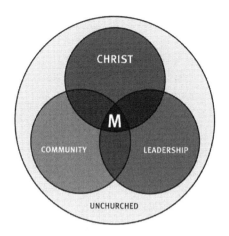

MISSION & MEMBERSHIP | WK 6

REVIEWING THE FOUR MISSIONAL RELATIONSHIPS

There is one body and one Spirit—just as you were called to the one hope that belongs to your call—one Lord, one faith, one baptism, one God and Father of all, who is over all and through all and in all.

- Ephesians 4:4-6

READ

What is membership and how does it intersect with being a missional community? Simply put, a member of Clear Creek Community Church is a person who commits to the church as missional community by proclaiming, "I belong! I support! I believe! I go!"

We understand there may be many who attend Clear Creek that don't have any desire for membership. For example, they may be new to the church or just investigating the claims of Christianity. To commit to missional community wouldn't be wise or prudent at the time. Please know that we are very grateful for you and your connection to CCCC. But there may be others who, through this study, realize they want to be counted among those who are committed to CCCC as a missional community. For them, that commitment is evidenced in membership.

While some churches may have complicated avenues for membership and others with little to no membership process at all, at Clear Creek Community Church, membership is simply the union of these four commitments. The New Testament teaches nothing more, nothing less. To be a member of the local church is to be committed to each of these relationships – Christ, church leadership, church community and the unchurched.

"I BELIEVE" – COMMITMENT TO CHRIST
- I place my faith in Jesus Christ alone for my salvation
- I have been baptized as a believer in Jesus Christ
- I affirm the essential beliefs of CCCC

"I SUPPORT" – COMMITMENT TO LEADERSHIP
- I support the mission, values, and strategy of CCCC
- I will yield to the elders in matters of doctrine, direction and discipline

"I BELONG" – COMMITMENT TO COMMUNITY
- I am in a CCCC small group
- I affirm the Gospel-Centered Growth process

"I GO" – COMMITMENT TO UNCHURCHED
- I invest in the unchurched and invite them to CCCC
- I pray for my Top 5

Indeed, to desire membership but embrace less than all four relationships will leave a person who wants to be a member in a less than productive position. Throughout the study, some sections have ended with a description of behavior contrary to the committed relationships and living missionally. In order to help you understand better how the commitment they offer falls short of being missional, they will be given titles.

- *The Rebel* – This person commits to community and to Christ but not the leadership. He wants to be a part of small group and engage in worship of Christ at a service but rejects the direction of the elders. He subordinates the mission, vision and values of the local church to his own personal mission and values. In the end, these individuals promote an *adversarial relationship* with the church, specifically with the church leadership, and can easily become the source of disputes, complaints and a disgruntled spirit in the congregation.

- *The Consumer* – This individual commits to Jesus in salvation and the mission, vision and values of the leadership, but doesn't want to be engaged in the church community. He resists or refuses fellowship, because to enter into community is to relinquish their power to control the terms of the relationship. In other words, these individuals have a *transactional relationship* with the church. This individual wants from the church what he refuses to give. He treats the church not as parishioner, but as consumer.

- *The Faker* –This person assumes since he is good at checking off a bunch of religious boxes he merits God's favor and salvation. As such, it is easy for him to commit church leadership because he finds his security in his ability to perform responsibilities, and it's also easy to commit to community because he is comfortable in religious environments where he compares his spirituality with other people. Unfortunately, these individuals are not truly seeking to grow their relationship with Christ and glorify God but to further personal agendas such as expanding their business clientele or search for a spouse. Ultimately, they have a *utilitarian relationship* to the church.

A WORD TO REBELS, CONSUMERS AND FAKERS
Rebels, *Consumers* and *Fakers* are people who desire membership at CCCC but adamantly and steadfastly reject commitment to one or more of the four relationships. Due to their unwilling spirit, they aren't ready for membership. Indeed, if through this study you identify with one of those categories we would humbly ask you to repent. Stop hurting yourself and the church. Flee from any type of non-missional relationship to the church (adversarial, transactional or utilitarian), and join others in committing to all four missional relationships – Christ, his local leadership, his local community and the unchurched. If you have no desire to *ever* make those commitments but still

want to become a member, both you and the leadership of CCCC will be frustrated.

DIFFERENT PLACES ON THE JOURNEY

We also realize that many cannot affirm these commitments not because of a desire to be contrary or disruptive, but simply because they are on a journey and not yet at a place where others may be. That's okay! Yes, you read that correctly. We are okay with the fact that you may not be where others are in the journey. In fact, we are incredibly excited that you have chosen to partner with us in learning more about what it is to become a fully devoted follower of Jesus Christ! Remember, these commitments are about membership at Clear Creek Community Church, not attendance at CCCC.

Just because someone isn't ready for membership doesn't mean they aren't wanted or welcome. They may be spiritual seekers who simply want to know more about Jesus and the gospel. Others may desire to better understand our mission and values. Still others may need more time dissecting our essential beliefs to see if that is what they believe. All of us are in process. None of us have arrived. What this tells us is that while some are ready and willing to embrace church membership, others may need more time in the journey. We welcome both groups of people!

Our hope is to journey together in such a gracious, truthful and loving way that we all have the greatest opportunity to become fully devoted followers of Jesus Christ.

IT'S ALL ABOUT THE MISSION

In the end, the church as missional community is ultimately about leading unchurched people to become fully devoted followers of Jesus Christ. If you desire to commit to Christ, the church community, the church leadership and reaching the unchurched, then consider partnering with us as a member!

SUMMARY – "MISSION AND MEMBERSHIP"

- Membership at Clear Creek Community Church is a commitment to four relationships – Christ, the leadership, the community and the unchurched.
- To embrace anything less than all four relationships is to fall short of the biblical commitment of membership for followers of Jesus.
- These commitments are about church membership not church attendance.
- We realize this is a journey. We provide this study and opportunity for membership in the hopes of better journeying together.

REFLECT

Take some time to reflect on the four relationships of membership and the commitments therein. You next group time will be spent reviewing the last five studies and the next steps to be taken. We also suggest you take time to read through the appendices to better acquaint yourself with the beliefs, policies and practices of Clear Creek Community Church.

1. Review the previous weeks and write down any questions, concerns or thoughts.

    _____

    _____

    _____

    _____

    _____

    _____

    _____

2. What are any "next steps" you believe you need to take?

    _____

    _____

_____

_____

_____

_____

_____

3. What questions do you have about membership
    that you feel weren't answered in this study?

_____

_____

_____

_____

_____

_____

_____

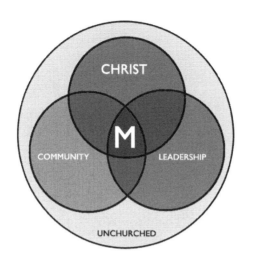

CHURCH MEMBERSHIP
AT CLEAR CREEK COMMUNITY CHURCH

APPENDICES

ESSENTIAL BELIEFS

The following are Clear Creek Community Church's essential beliefs *for membership*. In the essential beliefs we have unity, in the non-essential beliefs we have liberty, in all our beliefs we show charity. For a more detailed understanding of Clear Creek Community Church's *general* theological disposition we recommend *Systematic Theology* by Dr. Wayne Grudem.

About God
God is the Creator and Ruler of the universe. He has eternally existed in three persons: the Father, the Son, and the Holy Spirit. These three are coequal and are one God. Genesis I:1, 26, 27; 3:22; Psalms 90:2; Matthew 28:19; 1 Peter 1:2; 2 Corinthians 13:14

About Jesus Christ
Jesus Christ is the Son of God. He is co-equal with the Father. Jesus lived a sinless human life and offered Himself as the perfect sacrifice for the sins of all people by dying on a cross. He arose from the dead after three days to demonstrate His power over sin and death. He ascended to Heaven's glory and will return again someday to earth to reign as King of Kings, and Lord of Lords. Matthew 1:22, 23; Isaiah 9:6; Colossians 1:15-16

About the Holy Spirit
The Holy Spirit is co-equal with God the Father and the Son of God. He is present in the world to make men aware of their need for Jesus Christ. He also lives in every Christian from the moment of salvation. He provides the

Christian with power for living, understanding of spiritual truth, and guidance in doing what is right. He gives every believer at least one spiritual gift when they are saved. As Christians we seek to live under His control daily. 2 Corinthians 3:17; John 16:7-13, 14:16-17; Acts 1:8; 1 Corinthians 2:12, 3:16; Ephesians 1:13; Galatians 5:25; Ephesians 5:18.

About the Bible
The Bible is God's Word. It was written by human authors, under the supernatural guidance and inspiration of the Holy Spirit. It is the supreme source of truth for Christian beliefs and living. Because the Bible is inspired by God, it is the truth without any mixture of error. 2 Timothy 3:16; 2 Peter 1:20, 21; Proverbs 30:5; Psalms 119:105, 160.

About Human Beings
People are made in the spiritual image of God to be like Him in character. People are the supreme object of God's creation. Although every person has tremendous potential for good, all of us are marred by "sin" which separates people from God and causes many problems in life. Genesis 1:27; Psalms 8:3-6; Is. 53:6a; Romans 3:23; Isaiah 59:1,2.

About Salvation
Salvation is God's free gift to us, but we must accept it. We can never make up for our sins by self-improvement or good works. Only by trusting in Jesus Christ alone as God's offer of forgiveness can anyone be saved from sin's penalty. When we turn from our self-ruled life and turn to Jesus in faith alone, we are

saved. Eternal life begins the moment one receives Jesus Christ into his/her life by faith alone. Romans 6:23; Ephesians 2:8-9; John 14:6, 1:12; Titus 3:5; Galatians 3:26; Romans 5:1.

About Eternal Security

Because God gives us eternal life through Jesus Christ, the true believer is secure in that salvation for eternity. If one has been genuinely saved, he cannot lose it. Salvation is maintained by the grace and power of God, not by the self-effort of the Christian. It is the grace and keeping power of God that gives us this security. John 10:29; 2 Tim. 1:12; Hebrews 7:25, 10:10, 14; 1 Peter 1:3-5.

About Eternity

People were created to exist forever. We will either exist eternally separated from God by sin or eternally with God through forgiveness and salvation. To be eternally separated from God is hell. To be eternally in union with Him is eternal life. Heaven and Hell are real places of eternal existence. John 3:16; 1 John 5:11-13; Romans 6:23.

These statements of faith do not exhaust the extent of our beliefs. The Bible itself, as the inspired and infallible Word of God speaks with final authority concerning truth, morality, and the proper conduct of mankind, is the sole and final source of all that we believe. For purposes of Clear Creek Community Church's faith, doctrine, practice, policy, and discipline, our Teaching Elders are the Church's final interpretive authority on the Bible's meaning and application.

CREEK SPEAK

You may have been at CCCC and heard someone say something which caused you to ask, "What does that mean?" CCCC is its own culture, and like every culture, there our terms and sayings unique to that specific culture. We have listed some of them for you.

Disciple – someone who decides to follow Jesus by receiving him as Lord and Savior; also known as a Christian.

Fully Devoted Follower – a disciple of Jesus who is growing both in his or her identity as a citizen, family member, and missionary that results in the activity of listening and obeying, loving and serving, and going and multiplying.

Go Ops – missional service opportunities for small groups to engage in our community and the world.

Go Catalyst – a small group member who is responsible for identifying and coordinating Go Ops for the group.

Gospel – the "good news" that God has done for us (i.e., salvation) what we cannot do for ourselves through the Person and Work of Jesus Christ.

Group Guide – a person who oversees navigators with the purpose of providing leadership development, pastoral care, and ministry support.

GroupLink – an event (2-3 times a year) aimed at placing people into small groups.

GroupUp – an event which concludes the first six weeks of a small group with the intent of encouraging, celebrating and helping those in group with their commitments.

Host – a group member who shares in the leadership of the group by assuring that a suitable location and atmosphere for the group is provided.

Last 10% - the part of "speaking the truth in love" which is most difficult and uncomfortable to share with someone that would ultimately lead to their benefit.

Monday Conversation – a conversation or time of evaluation deferred to Monday when problems arise during a worship service (usually a Sunday) that cannot be addressed immediately, or when a conversation would hinder someone's service.

Navigator – the individual who leads a small group of others into community. They are small group leaders.

Navigator-In-Training (N.I.T.) – an identified small group apprentice who shares in the leadership of the group.

Seeker – a term for a non-believer who is investigating the person and work of Jesus Christ.

Spiritual Growth Grid – a chart showing how the gospel is to impact our devotion to Jesus by basing that devotion in who God is and what he is done for us in Christ. It is related to the gospel truth of that identity informs activity.

Spiritual Formation – the process by which believers are formed by the Holy Spirit into the likeness of Christ. This happens through our active cooperation with the Holy Spirit, and expresses itself in love and service toward God and others.

Top 5 – the list of unbelieving people for whom a believer is praying specifically and regularly; also called "most wanted" list or "people who matter" list.

Two Stickies – a term which embodies our value of "sanity" and refers to the maximum involvement limit of two small groups as a general guideline for individuals. The term came from a leadership meeting early in the church's history where each leader was given two sticky notes to put on an organizational chart.

Unchurched People – people who do not attend a church. The person may have 1) stopped attending church at an age of independence, 2) been turned-off by a previous church experience, or 3) have never attended a church.

Unholy Trinity - a relationship triangle created when a person complains or gossips to a third party instead of dealing directly with the person who caused an offense (according to the pattern of Matthew 18:15).

2AM Friends - friends that will be there for you in any situation at any time. This is the vision for the small group you "do life" with.

THE VALUES OF CLEAR CREEK COMMUNITY CHURCH

Naturally, because we are a collection of diverse individuals, we all have slightly different values with regard to how we go about serving Christ. Yet certain common values unify our efforts and define our community. The values were determined by the Elders and are expected to be around for at least 100 years. We use values to "filter" all CCCC decisions. If a proposed solution or decision does not clear these value filters, then it is not a decision or solution that will stand. These are the values Clear Creek Community Church lives by:

Gospel-Centered | It all starts with Jesus
Jesus came to tell us, and show us, that there's more to life—a life more fulfilling than any life apart from him. This life is available right now, today, and he's made a way for us to experience it. At Clear Creek, everything we do starts with the good news of what Jesus has done for us and the truth that following him changes us in real and lasting ways.

Biblical Community | We need each other.
The kind of life that Jesus offers isn't something that we were meant to experience alone. It's about being connected to other people who are also exploring the fullness of this life, and applying the gospel of Jesus to everyday life. As we walk through life together— through the good, the bad, the struggles, and the

celebrations—we discover a richness to life that only comes through relationships that matter.

Missional Living | We've got a job to do.
We aren't supposed to keep this discovery of a fuller life to ourselves. We demonstrate the power of following Jesus to the people and community around us by helping the needy, giving a hand to those who are struggling, and showing the love of Jesus to everyone we meet. That doesn't mean we don't talk about it also. It just means that we lead those around us by living out what it means to follow Jesus and follow it up with the story of how Jesus changes our lives. We want to show it clearly ... and then share it boldly.

Relentless Stewardship | We've got something to give.
The essence of this new life in Jesus is the act of giving. God gave His Son, Jesus, to do for us what we couldn't do for ourselves—to bring us into this new kind of life. How do we respond to that? What should that produce in our hearts and in our lives? We believe that if we're truly going to live out the fullness of this life, we've got to make constant strides in giving to others out of what God has given to us. When this kind of generosity takes hold in you, you'll respond by sharing in every way you can—in your time, in your skills and gifts, and even in your finances. At Clear Creek, we give because God is changing our hearts and inviting us to respond.

GOOD GROUP HABITS

1. **Always remember our purpose!** We are here to grow in full devotion to Jesus.

2. **We all have feelings** (even guys). When we talk to each other we should be mindful of HOW we say something, making sure we've phrased it in such a way that the people we're talking to have the greatest chance of receiving what we've said. Speak as you want to be spoken to. Let courtesy, grace, and respect win the day.

3. **Each small group member is *invited* but *not required* to join in the discussion.** The same can be said about prayer time and accountability. Yet even though it isn't required, to opt out of these things is a huge detriment to not only your spiritual growth but the group as well. It's been said that the less you open up, the less you grow. So take a chance and engage!

4. **On the flipside, don't be a "talk-hog".** Like a "ball-hog" in basketball who keeps the ball to himself, dominates the shot-taking, and never passes it to others, don't be the one who always has to talk every time the opportunity arises. Discussion time is limited, so please be sure that everyone who wants to speak has the opportunity

THE CHURCH: A MISSIONAL COMMUNITY

to do so (this applies to prayer time too). In other words, *"Pass the ball."*

5. **We're in this for the long haul.** If you've ever run a marathon or another long-distance race you know it all comes down to pacing yourself. Growth is the same way. We want to grow in Christ but that doesn't always come quickly, sometimes it takes time to get where we want to go...or where others know we should be. Belief changes are changes that usually take time as we're getting before truth, letting it soak in, and slowly owning it ourselves. That means process. That means time. So if we want group to work best we must be committed to being patient with each other. Not all of us are at the same place spiritually and frankly, all of us have weak areas spiritually that others may have down already. So let's create a patient and loving environment where someone can ask questions and feel safe, not threatened. Let's run together not in an *"I-can't-believe-you-don't-know-that"* way but an *"I-love-you-enough-to-let-us-find-the-truth-together"* way.

6. **Let's stay on-task.** It's easy to let group become an exercise in rabbit-chasing but time is short. While a rabbit or two maybe okay, the group should do its best on staying the course in what it is studying/discussing and how we can apply

what we're learning. The Group Navigator's job is to try to keep the ship sailing forward.

7. **When it comes to prayer time, share yourself.** Community suffers when the only prayer requests seem to be for "Aunt Bertha's bad toe" week after week. Let your group pray for you – your needs, your desires, and your heart.

8. **If you have to miss group, please let us know ahead of time.** Thanks!

9. **Do your homework if you have any!**

10. **"What happens in group stays in group."** Confidentiality is a must when it comes to sharing our hearts with each other! *NOTE*: A Navigator is accountable to a Group Guide. The Group Guide is considered a *member* of the group. Thus we consider a group's confidentiality intact if a Navigator divulges group-sensitive information in order to seek counsel from his/her Group Guide.

CHURCH DISCIPLINE POLICY

The mission of Clear Creek Community Church is to reach unchurched people and lead them to become fully devoted followers of Christ. The Elders of Clear Creek Community church are charged with promoting the mission of the church, and in so far as is possible, remove barriers to its accomplishment.

Scriptural principles of church discipline shall be applied to members and non-members who are identified as regular attenders when their actions or behaviors impede the Church in the accomplishment of its mission.

Discipline is an act of love, not vengeance or spite (Philippians 2:1-4, 1 John 4:7-8). The primary focus of the process is the restoration of the errant individual to fellowship with God and his Church (Galatians 6:1). Every effort will be made to understand the facts of the situation (Proverbs 18:13, 1 Thessalonians 5:14, James 1:19-20) and to follow the biblical disciplinary process outlined in passages such as Matthew 18:15-17; 1 Corinthians 5:1-5, 2 Corinthians 2:5-8 and Titus 3:10-11 in accordance with the bylaws of Clear Creek Community Church, Section 5.08.d.2.

The Purpose of Church Discipline
- To bring the sinning individual to repentance in order to restore fellowship with God and His church. (Galatians 6:1)

- To purify the church by removing from active participation those deliberately living in consistent disobedience to Biblical teachings (1 Corinthians 5: 12-13; 1 Peter 4:17). Such disobedience could include:

    i.   Sexual immorality (1 Corinthians 5)
    ii. Lawsuits (1 Corinthians 6:1-8)
    iii. Divorce and remarriage (Matthew 19:9)

Dr. Wayne Grudem notes,

On the other hand, there does not seem to be any explicit limitation specified for the kinds of sin that should be subject to church discipline. The examples of sins subject to church discipline in the New Testament are extremely diverse: divisiveness (Rom. 16:17; Titus 3:10), incest (1 Cor. 5:1), laziness and refusing to work (2 Thess. 3:6–10), disobeying what Paul writes (2 Thess. 3:14–15), blasphemy (1 Tim. 1:20), and teaching heretical doctrine (2 John 10–11).

Nonetheless, a definite principle appears to be at work: all sins that were explicitly disciplined in the New Testament were publicly known or outwardly evident sins, and many of them had continued over a period of time. The fact that the sins were publicly known meant that reproach was being brought on the church, Christ was being dishonored, and there was a real possibility that others would be encouraged to follow the wrongful patterns of life that were being publicly tolerated.[4]

- To correct actions or behaviors which are the cause of serious discord or dissent within the church body. (Romans 16:17-18; Proverbs 6:16-19).

- To prevent the spread of doctrines and practices contrary to those set out in the Clear Creek Community Church *Essential Beliefs* (Romans 16:17-18, 2 Thessalonians 3:6-15) or other doctrines the elders might specify.

Disciplinary Procedure

1. The errant individual shall first be confronted privately by a believer who has knowledge of the offense and is motivated by the spiritual welfare of the offender (Matthew 18:15).

2. If the individual does not repent and the offense continues, the concerned believer should confront the offender in the presence of one or two witnesses (Matthew 18:16). These witnesses should be people who are trustworthy and able to give reliable testimony (Deuteronomy 19:15; John 8:17; 2 Corinthians 13:1).

3. Should the individual continue in disobedience, the confronting believers shall take the matter to an

---

[4] Wayne Grudem, Systematic Theology, 896-897.

Elder. The Elder shall interview the persons making the allegation in order to ascertain the facts in the case and the reasons for the allegation. The Elder shall document the nature of the offense, verify that the correct Biblical process has been followed, and determine whether to bring the matter to the attention of the Elders as a whole. The written allegations should be signed and dated by the confronting believers.

4. The written allegations shall be presented to the Elder body. The Elders by consensus will decide whether to pursue the matter and, if warranted, appoint two or more of their body to investigate further.

5. The offending person will be given the opportunity to be interviewed by the appointed Elders and discuss the allegations. Notes should be kept of the meeting.

6. If, after due investigation, it is determined that there is merit in proceeding with a disciplinary process then the Elders will develop a restoration plan for the individual, a timeframe for the individual to demonstrate compliance with the plan, and specific disciplinary actions that will be taken if the plan is not complied with.

7. The person against whom the allegations have been made shall be notified in writing of a disciplinary meeting that will deal with the specific allegations. Elders will be appointed to meet with the person, give them a written description of the specific allegations, the disciplinary actions that the Elders

might pursue if the matter is not resolved in the timeframe agreed upon by the Elders, and a restoration plan. In an attempt to have the matter dealt with in a timely manner, the meeting should be scheduled within 30 days of the presentation of the written allegations to the Elder body.

On the other hand, if after due investigation there appears to be no reason for any further disciplinary action the matter shall be dropped. An Elder or Elders shall be appointed to counsel all parties involved and bring to an end any continuation of rumors or conflicts related to the matter. Both parties shall then be informed in writing that the investigation has been concluded and the allegations dismissed. A record of the investigation shall be kept in the Elders confidential records.

8. Whenever the sinning person demonstrates a spirit of repentance by acknowledgement of the sin, seeks forgiveness from God and the church, asks the forgiveness of the offended, and makes restitution where necessary, the Elders at their discretion may elect to fully restore the penitent to the fellowship of the church (2 Corinthians 2:5-11; Galatians 6:1).

9. If the sinning person has not repented within the time set by the Elders, disciplinary actions may be imposed by consensus of the Elder body. These actions could include some or all of the following: (Matthew 18:17b; 1 Corinthians 5:9-13) (See Section 5.08 of the Bylaws)

    a. Revocation of church membership.
    b. Removal from positions of leadership in the church.
    c. Removal from positions of service in the church.
    d. Barred from church fellowship, facilities, and functions.
    e. A public rebuke made before the congregation of CCCC. (1 Tim. 5:20)

10. A request for resignation of membership or any other voluntary severance from Clear Creek Community Church shall not automatically resolve the church from further responsibility in the matter. When a person under church discipline leaves Clear Creek Community Church to attend another church, the Elders shall determine whether to privately inform the leadership of the other church of the individual being under church discipline at Clear Creek Community Church.

11. All documentation of disciplinary actions shall be kept in the confidential Elders records.

One final note from Dr. Grudem on the matter of church discipline,

> There is always the need, however, for mature judgment in the exercise of church discipline, because there is lack of complete sanctification in all our lives. Furthermore,

when we realize that someone is already aware of a sin and struggling to overcome it, a word of admonition may in fact do more harm than good. We should also remember that where there are issues of conduct on which Christians legitimately disagree, Paul encourages a wide degree of tolerance (Rom. 14:1–23).[5]

This is a very serious and weighty practice. Therefore church discipline should be executed in a very careful manner with the knowledge of the sin kept to the smallest group possible and disciplinary measures increasing in strength until there is a solution.[6] Again, the aim of this biblical practice is loving restoration to Christ and his church.

***For the technical understanding of church discipline process, please refer to the CCCC Bylaws, Exhibit B.

---

[5] Ibid, 896-897.

[6] Ibid.

ELDERS' PERSPECTIVE ON BAPTISM

Baptism is the testimony that one has renounced the old life of self-centeredness and has begun a new life of following Jesus Christ as Savior and Lord. We view baptism as a practice of obedience to Jesus Christ. Baptism is a physical symbol of the spiritual reality of what Christ does in a believer's life. Christ baptizes a believer in the Holy Spirit (Matthew 3:11), cleanses a believer from sin (Acts 22:16), and gives the believer a new life—a resurrected life (Romans 6:3-4, Colossians 2:12). When one places faith in Jesus Christ, the believer should seek to be baptized as soon as possible as a way of obeying Jesus (Acts 8:36, Acts 16:33, Acts 18:8) and publicly proclaiming faith in Jesus. Baptism is so important that the New Testament assumes everyone who believes in Jesus will be baptized. Baptism is not essential to salvation (Titus 3:5, Luke 23:39-43).

In the New Testament, baptism always follows personal faith (Acts 2:38, Acts 2:41, Acts 8:12-13). We only baptize people who have personal faith in Jesus, therefore infants are not baptized. While infant baptism is often meaningful to parents, the person baptized did not experience scriptural baptism. Believers baptized as infants should seek New

Testament baptism after coming into a personal relationship with Jesus Christ by faith.

Baptism in the Bible is done by immersion. The word in the New Testament translated "baptism" actually means 'to immerse, or dip under. The New Testament seems to indicate Jesus was immersed in his baptism (Matthew 3:16). Only immersion adequately symbolizes death and resurrection (Romans 6:3-4, Colossians 2:12). Those who were baptized in some other way, other than immersion, are encouraged to seek baptism by immersion in keeping with the Biblical pattern. However, the mode of baptism (immersion, pouring or sprinkling) is not viewed as an essential matter for membership at Clear Creek Community Church.

ELDERS' PERSPECTIVE ON GIVING

A fully devoted follower of Christ recognizes that all of one's possessions come from God and belong to God (Psalm 24:1, 1 Chronicles 29:11-12). One manages resources faithfully according to the teachings of the Bible and the leadership of the Holy Spirit (1 Corinthians 4:2). God uses material resources and one's faithfulness to manage resources to develop character (Luke 16:10-11). Giving is a heart issue. We give, not because God needs the money, but because God directs the heart to give (Matthew 6:21). Giving is just one aspect of responsible management of material resources.

The local church is God's redemptive agent in the world (Matthew 16:18) and should be the primary recipient of a Christian's giving (2 Corinthians 9:11-12). Christians are also responsible to give to the poor (James 2:14-16, Matthew 25:34-35), to provide for aging parents (Exodus 20:12, Mark 7:10-13), to assist other Christians as needs arise (Acts 2:44-45, 1 John 3:17), and to support Christian causes as the giver feels led by the Holy Spirit (2 Corinthians 9:7).

While the Bible is primarily descriptive, rather than prescriptive, in how a follower of Jesus is to give, the Bible teaches a follower of Jesus to give systematically

(1 Corinthians 16:2, Proverbs 3:9-10), proportionately (1 Corinthians 16:2), generously (2 Corinthians 9:6), sacrificially (Matthew 12:41-44, 2 Corinthians 8:2-3) and faithfully (1 Corinthians 4:2) to the church for the work of God in the world.

How much is a Christian to give to the church? The only amount indicated in the Bible for regular giving is a tithe, or one tenth of one's income. Therefore, the historical reference point for faithful giving to the local church is the tithe (Leviticus 27:30-33, Deuteronomy 12:6-7, Deuteronomy 26:12, Malachi 3:10).

ELDERS' PERSPECTIVE ON DIVORCE AND REMARRIAGE

What the Elders Believe about Marriage, Gender and Sexuality

God immutably created each person as a male or female. Marriage is one man and one woman, for life, that is consummated in complementary sexual union that ultimately can lead to reproduction and thus human flourishing. Sexual intimacy should only occur between a man and a woman who are married to each other.

Additionally, the elders affirm the biblical understanding that:

- Marriage is a reflection of Jesus' relationship to the church
- Marriage is to be a lifetime commitment
- Marriage is to be with another follower of Jesus
- Marriage is to be with someone from the opposite sex

What the Elders Believe about Divorce

Divorce is never a part of God's original plan for marriage. Thus, repentance from sinful behaviors and reconciliation is the most God-glorifying path for those facing the possibility of divorce. Reconciliation highlights the gospel truth God has reconciled us to himself through Jesus Christ, thus we are to be reconciled to one another – especially those joined together in the covenant of marriage.

What the Elders Believe about Remarriage after Divorce

The Bible describes some specific situations where remarriage is permissible, (though remarriage is not required and may not be the best alternative.) The Bible teaches remarriage is permissible:

- where a spouse has died (Rom. 7:2-3)
- where divorce has taken place due to adultery and the offended spouse's heart is hardened to the point where they refuse to seek reconciliation (Mt. 19:3-9)
- where divorce has taken place because an unbelieving spouse deserts the believing spouse (1 Cor. 7:15)

Christ-loving, Bible-honoring, Gospel-centered leaders hold differing views on divorce and remarriage for situations not specifically described in the biblical text.

Requests for Remarriage

Therefore, requests for remarriage of a divorced person requires a presentation of the specific circumstances of the divorce. The request will be considered by a selection of elders before a decision is made.

What if an individual realizes he/she was divorced on unbiblical grounds but now has remarried?
The elders would counsel the individual to recognize God's Word concerning marriage and divorce, repent of any sin (e.g., seek to repair relationships hurt by your divorce, confess your sin to your ex-spouse, etc.) and honor God in their current marriage, trusting God's gracious work of forgiveness in the gospel.

ELDERS' PERSPECTIVE ON GENDER DYSPHORIA

All people are created in the image of God (Gen. 1:27) and thus, have intrinsic worth and dignity as his creation. Included in the goodness of creation is the human body. It is part of what it is to be human and to discover our true self.

Unfortunately, with the fall, sin has permeated all creation, including humanity (Gen. 3, Rom. 5:12-21, Rom. 3:23). Sin turned the harmony and union of creation to disharmony and confusion. (Rom. 8:20-21). Our physical bodies are subject to this brokenness (Rom. 7:24). One evidence is gender dysphoria, which can be defined as "the experiences of distress associated with the incongruence wherein one's psychological and emotional gender identity does not match one's biological sex."[7] We acknowledge there are people for whom gender identity conflicts are real.

Clear Creek Community Church desires to show compassion to those who struggle with gender dysphoria by coming alongside them to be an understanding ear and a voice of grace that beckons them to the redeeming work of God in Christ.

---

[7] Mark Yarhouse, *Understanding Gender Dysphoria*, (IVP Academic), 2015.

The gospel says that God, through the Cross of Jesus, is ultimately restoring creation from brokenness to wholeness. This includes human beings. Jesus Christ saves and redeems people. Through the gospel, Christ gives his followers a new and primary identity as a child of God; this new identity supersedes all other identity issues. God is transforming his people into the image of Jesus over time. We do not stay the same. Rather, in following Christ, we become more and more the person God designed us to be.

The church is an outpost of God's kingdom which exhibits the life, values, and vision of God's kingdom. Thus, CCCC affirms the truth that human identity is not self-determined but established by God through his means of creation, namely, people are born with a spirit and body. A part of the biblical picture for wholeness is the connection of one's gender with biology, not psychology. In other words, one's being either male or female is determined by birth not by how one feels about oneself at any particular time. God's saving plan includes reorienting people to this biblical understanding of gender.

Therefore, the message of CCCC as it concerns gender dysphoria is to point those who struggle with it to the redeeming and restoring work of the gospel where one's perceived gender identity may undergo the sanctifying process of coming back into conformity with one's biological-at-birth sex. We recognize this may be a long journey with numerous struggles, but it is the kind of path followers of Jesus walk in other areas of life where renewal and restoration is needed (Rom. 8:12-14, Col. 3:1-11).

Clear Creek Community Church also believes that maleness or femaleness is set at biological birth. Thus, the following will be limited to biological-at-birth genders:

- Gender-specific ministries (e.g., women's small group, men's retreat)
- Restroom usage
- Any event or practice that is gender-specific.

Our hope is not to burden those who wrestle with gender dysphoria, but to demonstrate life in Christ's kingdom, a life which seeks to reorient followers of Jesus to God's will in all things, including gender identity.

BYLAWS OF CLEAR CREEK COMMUNITY CHURCH
(Approved and Adopted on September 20, 2015)

ARTICLE I
Name and Principal Office

§1.01.   The name of the Corporation is *CLEAR CREEK COMMUNITY CHURCH*. This Corporation will be further referred to in the Bylaws as the "Church."

§1.02.   The Church maintains its principal office at 999 N. FM 270 also known as Egret Bay Blvd. North, League City, Texas.

§1.03.   The Elders of the Church shall have full power and authority to change the principal office from one location to another with a 2/3 majority vote.

§1.04.   This Article may be amended to state any change of this principal office location to state the new principal office location. This change will also be properly recorded with the Texas Secretary of State.

ARTICLE II
Definitions

§2.01.   **"Teams"** – The Church will need teams to handle various parts of its operations and functions to serve its stated purpose. The Elders have the authority to create and dissolve teams as it chooses.

§2.02. **"Elder"** – For purposes of these Bylaws, Elders are the members that make up the Board of Directors of the Nonprofit Corporation Clear Creek Community Church. Elders may be one or more category of Elders. The categories of Elders are Strategic Elders, Teaching Elders, and Campus Elders.

§2.03. **"Elders of the Church"** – For purposes of these Bylaws, Elders of the Church is equivalent to the Board of Directors in accordance with Business Organization Code Section 22.001(1). The Elders of the Church will be made up of at a minimum three (3) Elders.

§2.04. **"Member"** – Individuals as defined by Section 6 of these Bylaws.

§2.05. **"Trustee"** – For purposes of these Bylaws, Trustees are elected or reaffirmed by the members on an annual basis and serve at the discretion of the Elders as defined by Section 8 of these Bylaws.

§2.06. **"Articles of Incorporation"** – For purposes of these Bylaws, Articles of Incorporation also refers to Certificate of Formation and any amendments to the Articles of Incorporation or Certificate of Formation in accordance with the formation of a non-profit corporation in the Texas Business Organizations Code.

ARTICLE III
Purpose

§3.01. The purpose of the Church is to serve the religious purpose of leading unchurched people to become fully devoted followers of Jesus Christ.

ARTICLE IV
Statement of Faith

§4.01. The Clear Creek Community Church is supportive of these statements of faith which may be modified by a majority vote of the Elders of the Church and are attached as Exhibit A to these Bylaws. These statements of faith do not exhaust the extent of our beliefs. The Bible itself, as the inspired and infallible Word of God that speaks with final authority concerning truth, morality, and the proper conduct of mankind, is the sole and final source of all that we believe. For purposes of Clear Creek Community Church's faith, doctrine, practice, policy, and discipline, our Elder Body is the Church's final interpretive authority on the Bible's meaning and application.

ARTICLE V
Affiliation

§5.01. This Church is autonomous and maintains the right to govern its own affairs, independent of any outside control, recognizing, however, the benefits of cooperation with other churches, networks and denominations in a variety of activities; therefore may do so as it chooses.

ARTICLE VI
Membership

§6.01.   Membership in this Church shall consist of all persons who have met the qualifications for membership and are listed on the membership records.

§6.02.   Qualifications for membership include all of the following:

a.   A personal commitment of faith in Jesus Christ for salvation and Lordship; and

b.   Baptism as a proclamation of turning from their self-ruled life to a new life of following Jesus Christ as Lord and Savior; and

c.   Completion of the Church membership requirements as required by the Elders.

§6.03.   Nothing in this Article shall be construed as limiting the right of the Church to refer to persons associated with it or in attendance at Church functions as "Members." No such reference, however, shall constitute that any such person is a Member of this Church. A person is not a member of the Church unless they complete the qualifications and requirements of membership as described in Section 6.02 of these Bylaws.

§6.04.   The Church Secretary shall keep and maintain an accurate, updated list of Church Members.

§6.05.   Every Member shall have the right to vote on the following matters:

a.   the annual budget of the Church;

b.   the election or removal of the Trustees as provided for in Section 8.01 in the Bylaws;

c.   the merger or dissolution of the Church as provided for in the Bylaws; and

d.   affirmation of the Elders by a majority vote at a Membership meeting.

§6.06.   Each Member sixteen (16) years of age and older is entitled to one vote. Voting by proxy is prohibited.

§6.07.   Members shall be removed from the Church records for the following reasons:

a.   Death; or

b.   By personal request of the Member (including not renewing membership); or

c.   Dismissal by the Elders according to the disciplinary actions as defined by the Bylaws.

ARTICLE VII
Membership Meetings

§7.01.   Meetings of the Members shall be held at the principal office of the Church or at such other place or places within or outside of Texas as may be designated from time to time by the Elders and notice of such meetings will always be provided in accordance with these Bylaws.

§7.02.   An annual membership meeting of the Members shall be held at such time as determined by the Elders. Subject to §7.05 of this Article, any business may be conducted at this meeting.

§7.03.   Special meetings may be called at any time by the Elders, the Senior Pastor or the Executive Pastor for any purpose by giving notice to the Members in accordance with §7.04 of this Article.

§7.04.   Notice requirements for membership meetings include:

a.   **General Requirements**. Whenever Members are required or permitted to take any action at a meeting, a minimum of fourteen (14) days notice shall be given to Members prior to a meeting. Notification of membership meetings shall be given in any of the following manners which shall be deemed to be a reasonable method of calling a membership meeting:

1. Distribution of written material to the congregation in attendance at a weekend or mid-week service; or

2. Announcement of the meeting in the Church newsletter; or

3. Oral announcement to the congregation at a weekend or mid-week service; or

4. Delivery by United States mail, email or other electronic means to each Member identified in the membership records; or

5. Notification by telephone.

b. **Notice of Certain Agenda Items**. Approval by the Members of any of the following proposals is valid only if the notice specifies the general nature of the proposal:

1. Annual Budget of the Church;

2. Election, replacement or removal of the Trustees;

3. Merger or Dissolution of the Church; or

4. Affirmation of the Elders appointed by the Senior Pastor by a majority vote.

§7.05. Those Members present and voting at a meeting duly noticed and called shall constitute a quorum of the membership for the transaction of business.

ARTICLE VIII
Trustees

§8.01. The Elders shall designate the number of Trustees of the Church. The Trustees shall be elected by Members at the annual membership meeting based upon the recommendation of the Elders. Each Trustee shall be asked for a one year commitment subject to review, recommitment and re-election by the Church Members each subsequent year. Election shall be by 2/3 vote of the Members present. A Trustee may only be removed by a vote of 75% of the Members present.

§8.02. The Trustees shall have the following duties:

a. To determine the compensation of the Senior Pastor of the Church by a 2/3 vote of the Trustees who have been duly elected by the Members; and

b. Execute legal documents or purchase agreements on behalf of the Church only at the direction of the Elders.

ARTICLE IX
Elders and Deacons

§9.01. **Elders.** The authorized number of Elders shall not be less than three (3). The Elders shall be appointed by the Senior Pastor and affirmed by the Members at a membership meeting by a majority vote. Elders, including the Senior Pastor, can be removed only for cause by 75 % vote of all of the Elders for removal, but the vote must take place at a time which is prior to the end of the one year commitment.

§9.02. The Elders have no specific fixed term of office. Instead, each Elder, upon appointment, shall be asked for a one year commitment, at the end of that year this appointment is subject to review, and reappointment by the Senior Pastor, recommitment, and re-affirmation by the Church Members each subsequent year.

§9.03.   Elders shall meet the Biblical qualifications in 1 Timothy 3:1-7.

§9.04.   The Elders may fall into one or more categories as Strategic Elders, Teaching Elders, or Campus Elders

a.   **Strategic Elders**

1. **Team (minimum of three (3) Elders):**

(a)   Senior Pastor/President (Team Leader).

(b)   At least two (2) other Elders appointed by the Senior Pastor/President (based on the Elder's gifts and talents).

2.   **Duties and responsibilities of the Strategic Elders are:**

(a) Overall direction and ultimate oversight of the Clear Creek Community Church (church wide).

(b)   Subject to the provisions and limitations of

Texas law, and any limitations in the Articles of Incorporation and these Bylaws, the activities, business and affairs of the Church shall be conducted and all corporate powers shall be exercised by or under the direction of the Strategic Elders. The Strategic Elders are responsible for the direction, doctrine and discipline of the Church.

(c) Change the principal office of the Church in the State of Texas from one location to another, and designate any place within or outside the State of Texas for the holding of any meeting or meetings of the Members or Elders; and

(d) Adopt, make and use a corporate seal and alter the form of the seal; and

(e) Exercise all other powers conferred by the Texas Business Organization Code or other applicable laws.

b. **Teaching Elders.**

1. **Team.**

(a) Teaching Pastor (Team Leader) appointed by the Senior Pastor/President.

(b) At least two (2) Elders appointed by the Teaching Pastor (based on Elder's gifts and talents).

2. **Duties and responsibilities of Teaching Elders.**

(a) Oversee sound teaching and preserve pure doctrine across all ages, venues and campuses of the Clear Creek Community Church.

c. **Campus Elders.**

   1. **Team.**

   (a) Campus Pastor (Team Leader) appointed by the Senior Pastor/President.

   (b) Others as nominated by the specific Campus Pastor and approved by a 75% approval vote of all Strategic and Teaching Elders.

   (c) Campus Elders are selected for each individual campus, but will also be called upon to exercise the Joint Powers of the Elders as set out in Section 9.05.

   2. **Duties and responsibilities of Campus Elders.**

   (a) Support the Senior Pastor/President and the Campus Pastor.

   (b) Oversee the direction of the individual campus of the Clear Creek Community Church.

   (c) Provide spiritual discipline for the campus as outlined in the Bylaws of Clear Creek Community Church.

   (d) Align the campus to the Mission, Vision, Values and Beliefs of Clear Creek Community Church.

   (e) Oversee the Deacons of the campus where they serve as Campus Elder.

THE CHURCH: A MISSIONAL COMMUNITY

§9.05. **Joint Powers**. The Strategic Elders, Teaching Elders and Campus Elders of this Church have the following joint powers and each Elder shall exercise only one vote in any decision to:

1. Appoint the Senior Pastor/President by a 75% approval vote of all of the Elders; and

2. Remove the Senior Pastor/President for cause only by a 75% approval vote to remove by all of the Elders; and

3. Determine the disposition of all or substantially all of the assets of the Church in accordance with its 501c(3) purpose as stated in the Articles of Incorporation and in these Bylaws only by a 75% approval vote of all the Elders; and

4. Approve the merger or dissolution of the Church only by a 75% approval vote of all the Elders; and

5. Approve amendments to the Articles of Incorporation or Bylaws of the Clear Creek Community Church only by a 75% approval vote of all the Elders; and

6. Provide discipline on any campus in accordance with the Bylaws since any Elder may take part in the discipline procedure as needed or required by the Bylaws.

§9.06. **Deacons.** Campus Deacons shall meet the Biblical qualifications in 1 Timothy 3:8-13.

148

§9.07. The Campus Deacons (serve at each Campus, not as a collective group)

a. **Team.**

> 1. Campus Pastor appoints a Team Leader(s).
>
> 2. Others as appointed by the Campus Elders.

b. **Duties and responsibilities of Campus Deacons only.**

> 1. Support the Campus Pastor.
>
> 2. Shepherd the people of the campus as assigned by the Campus Elders.
>
> 3. The Campus Deacons do not have any powers, authority, or responsibility for the direction, doctrine and discipline of the Church which is controlled by the Elders.

ARTICLE X
Meetings of the Elders

§10.01. Regular or special meetings of the Elders may be held at any place within or outside the State of Texas that has been designated from time to time by all of the Elders. In the absence of such designation, meetings shall be held at the principal office of the Church.

§10.02. A regular or special meeting of the Elders may be held at any place consented to in writing by all of the Elders before the meeting. If such consents are given, they shall be filed with the minutes of the meeting.

§10.03.   Any meeting of the Elders, whether regular or special, may be held by conference telephone or similar communication equipment, as long as all Elders participating in the meeting can hear one another. All such Elders shall be deemed to be present in person at such meeting.

§10.04.   Regular meetings will be held at the discretion of the Senior Pastor or Elders. The minutes of the Elders shall be kept on file in the principal office of the Church.

§10.05.   Special meetings of the Elders are governed by the following:

a.   **Authority to Call**. Special meetings of the Elders may be called for any purpose and at any time by the Senior Pastor/President or any other Elder.

b.   **Notice**.

1. **Manner of Giving**. Notice of the time and place of special meetings shall be given to each Elder by one of the following methods: (a) by personal delivery of written notice; (b) by first class mail, postage prepaid; (c) by telephone communication, either directly to the Elder or to a person at the Elder's office or home who the person giving the notice has reason to believe will promptly communicate the notice to the Elder, or

(d) by facsimile to the Elder's home or office, or
(e) by email or other electronic means.

2. **Time Requirements**. Notices sent by first class mail shall be deposited in the United States mail at least four (4) days before the time set for the meeting. Notices given by personal delivery, telephone, facsimile or email or other electronic means shall be delivered, telephoned, or faxed to the Elder at least twenty-four hours before the time set for the meeting.

3. **Notice Contents**. The notice shall state the time and place for the meeting. However, the notice does not need to specify the place of the meeting if the special meeting is to be held at the Church's principal office. The notice does not need to specify the purpose of the meeting.

§**10.06**. A majority of the Elders must be present at a meeting duly called and noticed to constitute a quorum for the transaction of business. Every action taken or decision made by a majority of the Elders present at a meeting duly held shall be the act of the Elders, subject to the provisions of the Texas Business Organization Code.

§**10.07**. Any action required or permitted to be taken by the Elders may be taken without a meeting, if all of the Elders, individually, or collectively, consent in writing or by other electronic means to the action. Such action by written or other electronic means to consent shall have the same force and effect as the unanimous vote of the Elders. Such written consent or consents shall be filed with the minutes of the proceedings of the Elders.

ARTICLE XI
Officers

§11.01.　The Officers of the Church shall be comprised of the Senior Pastor as the President, the Executive Pastor as Vice-President, a Secretary, and a Treasurer. The Senior Pastor appoints the Vice-President, Secretary, and Treasurer. The Executive Pastor shall act as moderator in the absence of the Senior Pastor. In the absence of the Senior Pastor and the Executive Pastor, a moderator will be appointed by the Senior Pastor. The Senior Pastor is selected by the Elders.

§11.02.　A vacancy in any office because of death, resignation, removal, disqualification or any other cause shall be filled only in the manner prescribed in these Bylaws for regular appointments to that office. Such vacancies may be filled as they occur.

§11.03.　The term of office for each Officer other than the President shall be reaffirmed by the President at the end of each year. The President may also choose to remove or replace any Officer at his discretion. Officers may serve for additional terms as provided for in this section.

§11.04.　The Senior Pastor/President may be removed for cause only by a 75% approval vote to remove by all of the Elders.

ARTICLE XII
Indemnification And Insurance

§12.01.　**Right to Indemnification of Elders, Officers**

and Trustees. Subject to any limitations and conditions in these Bylaws and/or the Articles of Incorporation, including, without limitation, this Article XII, each person who was or is made a party or is threatened to be made a party to or is involved in any threatened, pending or completed action, or other proceeding, whether civil, criminal, administrative, arbitrative or investigative (referred to in Article XII as a "Proceeding," which term also includes any appeal of such a Proceeding or any inquiry or investigation that could lead to such a Proceeding), by reason of the fact that he or she is or was an Elder or Officer or Trustee of the Church, or while an Elder or Officer or Trustee of the Church, shall be indemnified by the Church to the fullest extent permitted by Title 1, Chapter 8 of the Texas Business Organizations Code, as the same exists or may later be amended (but, in the case of any such amendment, only to the extent that such amendment permits the Church to provide broader indemnification rights than said law permitted the Church to provide prior to such amendment) against any and all judgments (including penalties, such as, but not limited to excise and similar taxes and fines) and against any and all expenses (including attorneys' fees and costs of settlements, provided such settlements are approved by the Church) that are reasonable and actually incurred by such person in connection with such Proceeding. Indemnification under this Article XII shall apply to a person who has at any time served in a capacity that entitles such person to indemnity under the terms of this Article XII even if such service occurred prior to the adoption of this Article XII and even if such person has ceased to serve in such capacity prior to the final disposition of the pertinent Proceeding. **It is specifically acknowledged that the indemnification provided in this Article XII expressly provides for indemnification for**

joint, sole or concurrent negligence or strict liability of any Officer or Elder or Trustee while acting in his or her official capacity or at the request of the Church as set out in this Article XII, and it is further specifically acknowledged that this bold faced and underscored text is a conspicuous notice. Any person entitled to indemnification pursuant to this Article XII is sometimes referred to here as an "Indemnified Person." No subsequent amendment of this Article XII shall terminate, limit or otherwise adversely affect the rights of any Indemnified Person with respect to indemnification as to any Proceedings regarding acts, omissions or events occurring prior to such amendment.

§12.02. Standard of Conduct. The standard of conduct for indemnification requires, as applicable, that the person to be indemnified:

a.   Acted in good faith, and

b.   Reasonably believed that his or her conduct on behalf of the Church, in his or her official capacity, was in the Church's best interests; in any case other than acting in an official capacity, that his or her actions were not opposed to the Church's best interests; and in the case of criminal proceedings, that he or she did not have reasonable cause to believe that his or her conduct was unlawful.

§12.03. An action taken or omitted by an Elder or Officer or Trustee with respect to an employee benefit plan, in performance of the person's duties for a purpose reasonably believed to be in the interest of the participants and beneficiaries of the plan is for a purpose that is not opposed to the best interests of the Church.

§12.04. A person does not fail to meet the standard for indemnification under this Article XII solely because of the determination of a proceeding by judgment, order, settlement, conviction or a plea of nolo contendere or its equivalent unless otherwise specifically set out in Section 1(c) of this Article XII.

§12.05. **Indemnification Not Permitted**. Indemnification is not permitted under this Article XII of a person who is found liable to the Church or is found liable because the person improperly received a personal benefit or who is convicted of a criminal act and:

a.   Does not include a judgment, a penalty, a fine, and an excise or similar tax, and

b.   May not be made in relation to a proceeding in which the person has been found liable for:

1. willful or intentional misconduct in the performance of the person's duty to the Church including any criminal act;

2. breach of the person's duty of loyalty owed to the Church; or

3. an act or omission not committed in good faith that constitutes a breach of duty owed by the person to the Church.

§12.06. For purposes of this Article XII, a person is considered to have been found liable in relation to a claim, issue or matter only if the liability is established by an order, including a judgment or decree of a court and all appeals of the order are exhausted or foreclosed by law.

§12.07. **Authorization of Indemnification.** Any indemnification under this Article XII (unless ordered by a court) shall be made by the Church only as authorized in the specific case upon a determination that indemnification of the present or former Elder, Officer or Trustee is proper in the circumstances because such person has met the applicable requirements set forth in Section 1 of this Article XII. Such determination shall be made with respect to a person who is an Elder or Officer or Trustee at the time of such determination, (i) by a majority vote of the Elders who are not parties to such action, suit or proceeding, even though less than a quorum, (ii) by a team of such Elders designated by majority vote of such Elders, even though less than a quorum, or (iii) if there are no such Elders or if such Elders so direct, by independent legal counsel in a written opinion. However, mandatory indemnification is required to the extent that an Elder or Officer or Trustee of the Church has been successful on the merits or otherwise in defense of any action, suit or proceeding described above, or in defense of any claim, issue or matter within such action, suit or proceeding, and such person shall be indemnified against expenses (including attorneys' fees) actually and reasonably incurred by him or her in connection with such action, suit or proceeding, or such claim, issue or matter within such action, suit or proceeding, without the necessity of authorization in the specific case.

§12.08. **Appearance as a Witness.** Notwithstanding any other provision of this Article XII, the Church may pay or reimburse expenses incurred by an Indemnified Person in connection with his or her appearance as a witness or other participation in a Proceeding at a time when he or she is not a named defendant or respondent in the Proceeding.

§12.09. **Insurance**. The Elders by a majority vote, may adopt a resolution authorizing the purchase and maintenance by the Church of insurance, at its expense, to protect itself or any Indemnified Person, whether or not the Church has or would have the power to indemnify such person against such expense, liability or loss under Article XII.

§12.10. **Savings Clause**. If this Article XII or any portion hereof shall be invalidated on any ground by any court of competent jurisdiction, then the Church shall nevertheless indemnify and hold harmless each Indemnified Person as to any and all judgments (including penalties, such as but not limited to excise and similar taxes and fines) and against any and all expenses (including attorneys' fees and costs of settlements, provided such settlements are approved by the Church) that are reasonable and actually incurred by such person in connection with such Proceeding, to the full extent permitted by any applicable portion of this Article XII that shall not have been invalidated and to the fullest extent permitted by applicable law.

ARTICLE XIII
Dissolution/Termination of Non-Profit Corporation

§13.01. **Dissolution/Termination Vote**. The Elders by a 75% affirmative vote of all the Elders to dissolve or terminate the Church after the Members have already approved dissolution or termination by a 2/3 majority vote.

§13.02. **Distribution of Church Assets.** In accordance with Section 22.304 of the Business Organization Code after all liabilities and obligations of the Church in the process of winding up are paid, satisfied and discharged in accordance with Chapter 11 of the Business Organizations Code, the property of the Church shall be applied and distributed as follows:

a.   Church property shall be returned, transferred or conveyed, if there is a written condition requiring return, transfer or conveyance of property upon the winding up, dissolution or termination of the Church and only in accordance with such a requirement, and

b.   The remaining Church property shall be distributed only for tax exempt purposes to one or more 501(c)(3) non-profit corporations established for the same or similar purposes as the Church unless the Articles of Incorporation or Certificate of Formation provide otherwise.

ARTICLE XIV
Records and Reports

§14.01.   The Church shall maintain the following records and reports:

a.   Accurate books and records of accounts (financial records);

b.   A record of property and assets owned by the Church including any deeds;

c.   Written minutes of the proceedings of its Members

and Elders;

d.   A record of the Members of the Church, setting forth the Members' names and addresses;

e.   Contribution statements for contributors; and

f.   Copy of all Bylaws and Articles of Incorporation.

§14.02. All such records shall be kept at the Church's principal office.

ARTICLE XV
Church Discipline/Dispute Process for Members and Non Members

§15.01.   **Purpose**. In the event any act or behaviors by any member or non-member occurs or a dispute is brought by any members that impedes the Church's religious purpose which is leading unchurched people to become fully devoted followers of Jesus Christ, the following steps of discipline/dispute may be followed by the Church, as listed in the nine (9) step disciplinary process as defined in Exhibit B.

ARTICLE XVI
Amendments to the Bylaws

§16.01. These Bylaws or any provision of them may be altered, amended or repealed by 75% approval vote of all of the Elders of the Church.

Duly adopted and approved, by which witness my hand and signature on same date.

Date _____

Secretary _____

EXHIBIT A

a. **About God**.

God is the Creator and Ruler of the universe. He has eternally existed in three persons: the Father, the Son, and the Holy Spirit. These three are co-equal and are one God. Genesis I:1, 26, 27; 3:22; Psalms 90:2; Matthew 28:19; 1 Peter 1:2; 2 Corinthians 13:14

b. **About Jesus Christ**.

Jesus Christ is the Son of God. He is co-equal with the Father. Jesus lived a sinless human life and offered Himself as the perfect sacrifice for the sins of all people by dying on a cross. He arose from the dead after three days to demonstrate His power over sin and death. He ascended to Heaven's glory and will return again someday to earth to reign as King of Kings, and Lord of Lords. Matthew 1:22, 23; Isaiah 9:6; Colossians 1:15-16

c. **About the Holy Spirit**.

The Holy Spirit is co-equal with God the Father and the Son of God. He is present in the world to make men aware of their need for Jesus Christ. He also lives in every Christian from the moment of salvation. He provides the Christian with power for living, understanding of spiritual truth, and guidance in doing what is right. He gives every believer at least one spiritual gift when they are saved. As Christians we seek to live under His

THE CHURCH: A MISSIONAL COMMUNITY

control daily. 2 Corinthians 3:17; John 16:7-13, 14:16-17; Acts 1:8; 1 Corinthians 2:12, 3:16; Ephesians 1:13; Galatians 5:25; Ephesians 5:18.

d.   **About the Bible**.

The Bible is God's Word. It was written by human authors, under the supernatural guidance and inspiration of the Holy Spirit. It is the supreme source of truth for Christian beliefs and living. Because the Bible is inspired by God, it is the truth without any mixture of error. 2 Timothy 3:16; 2 Peter 1:20, 21; Proverbs 30:5; Psalms 119:105, 160 3:26.

e.   **About Human Beings**.

People are made in the spiritual image of God to be like Him in character. People are the supreme object of God's creation. Although every person has tremendous potential for good, all of us are marred by "sin" which separates people from God and causes many problems in life. Genesis 1:27; Psalms 8:3-6; Is. 53:6a; Romans 3:23; Isaiah 59:1,2.

f.   **About Salvation**.

Salvation is God's free gift to us, but we must accept it. We can never make up for our sins by self-improvement or good works. Only by trusting in Jesus Christ alone as God's offer of forgiveness can anyone be saved from sin's penalty. When we turn from our self-ruled life and turn to Jesus in faith alone, we are saved. Eternal life begins the moment one receives Jesus Christ into his/her life by faith alone. Romans 6:23; Ephesians 2:8-9; John 14:6, 1:12; Titus 3:5; Galatians 3:26; Romans 5:1.

g.   **About Eternal Security**.

Because God gives us eternal life through Jesus Christ, the true believer is secure in that salvation for eternity. If one has been genuinely saved, he cannot lose it. Salvation is maintained by the grace and power of God, not by the self-effort of the Christian. It is the grace and keeping power of God that gives us this security. John 10:29; 2 Tim. 1:12; Hebrews 7:25, 10:10, 14; 1 Peter 1:3-5.

h.   **About Eternity**.

People were created to exist forever. We will either exist eternally separated from God by sin or eternally with God through forgiveness and salvation. To be eternally separated from God is hell. To be eternally in union with Him is eternal life. Heaven and Hell are real places of eternal existence. John 3:16; 1 John 5:11-13; Romans 6:23.

EXHIBIT B

Discipline/Dispute Process.

1. A discipline/dispute team of three (3) Church Members (the "Team") selected by the Campus Pastor may be contacted by any Member of the Church to hear a dispute or a request for disciplinary action which may involve any Member or non-member. At least one (1) member of the Team shall be an Elder selected by the Campus Pastor.

2. The Team will retain their positions unless they (i) voluntarily resign, or (ii) are replaced at the discretion of the Campus Pastor. Any open positions will be filled by the Campus Pastor.

3. Any Church Member or non-member may bring a dispute or request for a disciplinary action to the Team by requesting a meeting in writing (electronic or otherwise).

4. The Team will meet with the person or persons initiating the dispute or requesting the disciplinary action and also with the Member/non-member who is the subject of the dispute or disciplinary action.

5. The Team, after these meetings, may try to resolve the dispute or request for a disciplinary action informally by further discussion as agreed by all the Team Members.

6. If the dispute/disciplinary action request cannot be resolved, then the Team will notify the Campus Pastor.

7. After the Campus Pastor has been informed the dispute/disciplinary action cannot be resolved, the Campus

Pastor shall select at least two (2) Elders who shall interview the person or persons initiating the dispute or requesting disciplinary action and the Member or non-member who is the subject of the dispute or disciplinary action (offending person).

8. The two (2) Elders shall determine if any further action is needed and whether this should be presented to all the Elders for review. If no further action is needed the matter will be dismissed and the parties notified <u>in writing</u> (electronic or otherwise) as to the dismissal by the Elders.

9. **Restoration Team/Final Resolution**. If further action is required, the two (2) Elders will present the issue to all of the elders who will decide whether to pursue the matter and if necessary appoint a Restoration Team ("RT") to investigate the matter and reach a final decision. The RT will consist of Elders or individuals designated by the Elders to investigate the matter. The RT shall take the following actions:

    a.   The person who brought the dispute or requested disciplinary action and the person who is the subject of the dispute or disciplinary action will be notified by the RT <u>in writing</u> (electronic or otherwise) that there will be an investigation;

    b.   An investigation will be conducted by the RT, including but not limited to interviews with the persons involved and any witnesses; and

    c.   After the investigation, the RT may take some or all of the following actions to resolve the dispute or disciplinary action at their discretion:

1.   The matter will be dismissed, or

2.   The offending person's Church membership may be revoked;

3.   The offending person will be removed from Church leadership;

4.   The offending person will be barred from the Church fellowship;

5.   The offending person will be prohibited from the observation of the Last Supper;

6.   RT will counsel or hold a discussion with the persons involved to reach a final agreed resolution; or

7.   In addition to any disciplinary or dispute resolution or action, a plan may be established and agreed to in writing by the offending person and the RT or persons involved in any dispute. This plan will be monitored by the RT and the progress reported to the Elders.

d.   If there appears to be no reason for any disciplinary action or dispute resolution or other actions, both the requesting person and the person who is the subject of the dispute or request for disciplinary action shall be informed in writing (electronic or otherwise) that the investigation is concluded. The RT shall caution the persons involved that there should be no further discussions of this matter to protect the privacy of those persons involved.

e.   A record of any investigation, disciplinary action or dispute resolution shall be kept in the Elders' confidential records.

f.   A decision by the Elders or their designated RT, in all disciplinary or dispute resolution actions and dismissals shall be final.

Made in the USA
Columbia, SC
15 September 2022